14.50

TX
946.5   Warner, Mickey
,W37   Industrial foodservice
          and cafeteria management

Industrial Foodservice
and
Cafeteria Management

Industrial Foodservice
and
Cafeteria Management

MICKEY WARNER

Jule Wilkinson, Editor

Published by
INSTITUTIONS/VOLUME FEEDING MAGAZINE
Chicago, Ill.

Distributed by
Cahners Books, 89 Franklin St., Boston, Mass. 02110

Library of Congress Catalog Card No. 72-92378

ISBN-08436-0563-4

Printed in the United States of America

DEDICATION

This book is dedicated to my son Frank, and all young people of America, in whom I have an everlasting faith that they will continue to make and keep our country the true land of opportunity.

PREFACE

For many years I have been concerned about the lack of a book that would provide the young foodservice manager, or foodservice student, with the basic understanding of management that is required in the industrial foodservice business. In 1967 I became involved in preparing some material for presentation at New York City Community College, where I became associated with Mr. Alfred Goldsmid.

Some years later in 1971, Mr. Goldsmid encouraged me to prepare a course and present it at the Culinary Institute of America, and also encouraged me to write this book. Others at the Institute who provided encouragement, assistance and guidance: Mr. Jacob Rosenthal, Mr. Joseph Amendola, Mrs. Felicia De Angelis, Mr. Herman Glazer and Mr. David Geller all share a measure of credit for its completion.

The purpose of this book is to open the door for the foodservice student to the vast area of industrial foodservice opportunities. It is my fondest hope that our foodservice schools and colleges will place more emphasis in the future on this segment of the foodservice (hospitality) industry and thereby provide the nation's plants and factories, schools and hospitals and all the other "industrial" foodservice operations with a continuing flow of well qualified management personnel.

TABLE OF CONTENTS

LIST OF ILLUSTRATIONS

I: An Introduction to Industrial Foodservice

As today's foodservice management student prepares himself to become part of a management team in the foodservice industry, and as he nears the completion of his training and approaches the day when he will be seeking his first job, he reaches the point where he must decide in which part of the industry he wishes to specialize. In other major educational fields, a student selects a "major" subject and completes his education by specializing in that "major." For example: The engineering student becomes a chemical, civil, electrical or other type of engineer. The business student "majors" in accounting, personnel, finance or another specialized field of business. Other segments of education direct the student similarly.

In the past, food management schools have sometimes neglected to encourage their students to make a decision in advance as to which segment of this industry appeals to them and then to prepare themselves to enter that area of the industry. Selecting an area of the foodservice field and preparing oneself to excell in it is just as important in this industry as in any other.

Various major categories do exist in the foodservice field. Although they have as a common denominator the preparation and service of food to a customer, great variations do exist in "where" and "why" the service is performed. A hotel or motel provides one service, while a fast food operation provides a completely different service. By the same token, industrial foodservice operations exist for one purpose while commercial foodservice operations exist for another. (In Chapter III in the discussion of profit vs. productivity this difference is explained in further detail.)

The purpose of this book is twofold: (1) to give the foodservice/lodging student a basic understanding of the industrial foodservice phase of the industry and (2) to provide him with the basic management knowledge necessary for success as a manager in that field.

Entry Jobs to Industrial Feeding

In the industrial foodservice field, one of the primary entry jobs is as a chef-manager. In this position, the chef is in complete charge of the management of the foodservice as well as fully responsible for the preparation of the food requirements of the full menu. Needless to say, the chef who wishes to be successful and prosperous in the industrial foodservice field must know and understand the basics of industrial foodservice management.

Whether he is a chef-manager of a small industrial foodservice, or a chef in a larger industrial foodservice where there is an administrative manager, he is still part of the management team and his success can well be governed by his knowledge of management.

Segments of the Industrial Foodservice Field

Modern industrial foodservice is now a major segment of the mass feeding industry. In recent years, the "industrial caterer" has grown from the early stages of being a "regional company" to become a national organization that serves all parts of business, industry, government, educational and health institutions and many other places where large numbers of people gather as employees, students or residents.

Modern industrial foodservice is "big business" and, as is the case with all big business, is becoming a science. Basic business principles that are being taught in the nation's universities and business administration schools are now being applied in the Industrial Foodservice Field.

Industrial foodservice, as it is known today, falls into four basic categories:
1) Plants and factories in both urban and rural areas
2) Office buildings in and near large cities
3) Schools and colleges
4) Hospitals, nursing homes and similar institutions

Each category has its own special requirements and problems and each has its own specialists. All have one thing in common however, and that is that the foodservice is provided for a purpose other than to make a profit (although many do). That purpose changes with the area or institution.

A survey by *Inplant Magazine* in 1960 showed at that time that 50 per cent of all institutional or industrial foodservices were operated by the company, and 50 per cent were operated by contracted caterers. Although no recent figures are available, it is safe to say that 70 per cent are now operated by contracted caterers.

As students of foodservice management, in the early stages of shaping your careers, it is wise to learn something about all four areas of industrial foodservice and about both types of management—company and caterer operated.

Where It All Began

Some knowledge of the beginning of things is helpful in every field of endeavor. An old man once told me, "If you want to know where you're going, just look back and see where you have been, and compare." Looking back at the beginning of industrial food service and comparing it to today's operations can well tell us what the tomorrow of industrial foodservice will be.

It all began when the first cave man found a helper and fed and housed him. The helper did not receive a wage, but was reimbursed with protection, shelter, and *food*. As civilization progressed, men gathered in groups, forming villages, towns and cities, and they developed trades as a means of a livelihood. Later the craftsmen formed guilds and began to teach their trades or crafts to apprentices. These apprentices, as employees, were fed on the job, and industrial foodservice was born. As the great civilizations formed armies and marched against each other, special segments within the armies were utilized to feed the massed groups. This was one of the earliest examples of mass feeding and quantity cooking.

The great construction projects of history had their own examples of industrial foodservice to provide for the thousands of slaves used at each location. The building of the pyramids, the Roman roads, irrigation of the Nile Valley and other similar construction projects all required a planned foodservice for large numbers of "employees."

In America, early farmers had hired hands who were fed—the great western plains gave birth to the chuckwagon to feed the ranchers and their employees on location; railroads had an organized foodservice for their road gangs and the timber giants had an organized foodservice to meet the needs of their crews out in the forests.

As the Industrial Revolution developed, people began to mass in central locations to produce a single product in large quantities for one employer. The guilds of craftsmen who worked individually gave way to groups of craftsmen working collectively. General working conditions and eating conditions in factories in the late 1700's and early 1800's were deplorable.

Around 1800, Robert Owen was operating a mill in Scotland. Believing that better working conditions would produce a better employee who would then manufacture a better product, he opened a large "eating room" for his employees. This was merely a place set aside for eating food brought by the employee, with a place to prepare his beverage. That was the beginning of the "employee cafeteria" as it is known today.

The "cafeteria" arrived on the scene in 1891 in an operation begun by the Young Women's Christian Association (YWCA) in Kansas City. That group combined some of the self-service principles they had seen at the Ogontz Lunch Club for Young Women, in Chicago, with features of their own. Their purpose was to provide working girls living at the Association with good, low-cost meals. They called their new service a "Cafeteria," from the Spanish term meaning "a place where coffee is sold at retail."

Early Industrial Foodservice in the United States

Early cafeterias were located primarily in YMCA's and in YWCA's to feed the worker away from the job, but in 1902 the Plymouth Cordage Co. of Plymouth, Mass. installed the first cafeteria to be used for employee foodservice. Up until that time, employee foodservices were either of the lunch room type or a table service dining room.

The earliest known industrial foodservice in the United States (one that is still in operation) is the Bowery Savings Bank of New York. Meals are still served, with waitress service, without cost, and have been since 1834. Banks were among the earliest employers to provide foodservice to their employees and, in most cases, the meals were served free. Various telephone companies, which merged into the giant communications combines of today, were also pioneers in employee foodservice.

Since its inception, food provided by an employer for his employees, has been subsidized. In many cases, meals were served free. In many, the employer provided the space, equipment and labor, recovering from its sale price only the cost of the food; in effect, a

100 per cent food cost.

The practice of subsidizing the employee foodservice is still prevalent. It is the rare case where the employee foodservice recovers 100 per cent of its cost, as is the case in commercial foodservice. This subsidizing of employee meals is now an accepted practice in American business.

Employee cafeteria prices are often a part of the labor agreement between the trade union and the employer. A recent case involving an employer who raised the price of coffee in the cafeteria from 5¢ to 10¢ was brought by the employees to the National Labor Relations Board. The eventual ruling was that the subsidized cup of coffee was past practice and, therefore, the employees' just right; the employer was ordered to reduce the price of coffee from 10¢ to 5¢ or adjust the employees' wages accordingly.

Numerous cases exist where the subsidized meal has been ruled "part of wages" and, therefore, must remain. Some examples of early subsidized industrial feeding in America are:

The National Cash Register Co. of Dayton, Ohio in 1891. Service began for department heads and expanded to "Soup and Sandwich" for women employees.

Metropolitan Life Insurance in New York City. Service began in 1893.

Prudential Insurance, Newark, N. J. Started an employee foodservice in 1895.

New York Telephone Company. Began its first foodservice in 1891 and expanded to over 400 facilities as it became part of the Bell System.

The United Fruit Company. Has fed and housed its employees in many countries since 1900.

Arabian American Oil Company (ARAMCO) and other major oil companies have fed their employees at remote locations for many years.

The Industrial Caterer

In 1904, M. W. Cease and his brother, W. M. Cease, opened a cafeteria in the American Locomotive Works at Dunkirk, N. Y. A few years earlier, one of the brothers had quit working in the American plant in Richmond, Va., to sell lemonade to its workers. Today, Cease Commissary still exists in Dunkirk as part of the Interstate United Corporation. Other early industrial caterers came on the scene as regional companies, confining their efforts frequently to the type of industry in their immediate locale.

Fred B. Prophet was organized in Detroit and became a national company. Andrew and Francis Crotty formed a catering company in Boston that operated as far west as Texas.

Harding-Williams grew out of the John P. Harding Restaurant Company in Chicago in 1942. Harding's two sons teamed up with Ken L. Williams to form their company.

The Automatic Canteen Company gave birth to Nationwide Food Service in 1940, which then became a separate company.

In college feeding, John H. Slater, an English teacher at the University of Pennsylvania, took over the management of a fraternity dining room. This effort grew into one of the largest foodservice organizations in America.

At the time of World War I, about one-half of the major companies in America were providing some type of employee foodservice and over 85 per cent were company-operated. Today, over 70 per cent of all company-provided foodservices are caterer-operated.

Merger with Vending

About 1955, a couple of young men invented the fresh-brew coffee machine and industrial foodservice through vending was born. With the advent of a decent cup of vended coffee, machine-made and dispensed, a whole new market opened up to the industrial caterer. Oddly enough, few food service companies became vending companies or even showed an interest in vending. The impetus came as the new vending companies wanted foodservice support and began to buy or merge with foodservice companies. Today, most industrial caterers are food and vending service companies and some of them are classed among the top ten of the nation's 400 largest companies. Some have specialized in schools and colleges: some in hospitals; but most cover all four major areas of industrial foodservice. Some of the larger companies in the industry today, operating by and large on a national basis, are:

Automatic Retailers of America (ARA)   Saga Food Service
Canteen Corporation   The Macke Company
Interstate United Corporation   Servomation

Other large national and smaller regional companies exist and the above list is by no means complete. Mergers of companies and acquisitions of smaller companies by larger ones change the group at regular intervals.

Tomorrow's Picture for Industrial Foodservice

As the business world has become a world of specialists, the industrial caterer has joined the ranks as a specialized service company. While a good many plants, office buildings, schools and hospitals still operate their own facilities, the trend toward taking the busy executives of those industries out of the food business, thus allowing them more time to manage the businesses they are in, is accelerating.

At the same time, the top industrial catering companies are becoming more sophisticated. They are organizing their companies with divisions of Business and Industry; Hospitals and Institutions; and Schools and Colleges. They are doing research on new and better ways to freeze, reconstitute and mechanically serve food, facing the challenge of providing ever better foodservice to industry.

The successful industrial foodservice operator is learning modern management techniques; the use of the computer; methods of budgeting and how to coordinate his efforts with his "client" or "firm."

The industrial catering company of tomorrow will be as much a part of the technological field as the space age. As man and his work environment change, the industrial caterer will keep pace and change with it.

Future Outlook for the Chef-Manager

Tomorrow's picture indicates that the Chef-Manager of today will become the industiral foodservice manager of the larger operations. Basic food preparation skills are becoming less and less available as the American public settles for more and more "standardized" foods; and more and more back-of-the-house employees will have less and less basic knowledge of food production. The manager who also knows how to prepare and direct the preparation of good food will be the successful industrial foodservice manager of tomorrow.

II: The Four Fields

While the four basic fields of industrial foodservice, outlined in Chapter I, all have common management concepts and philosophies and are grouped under the heading "Industrial Foodservice," they differ greatly as to who is fed what, why and where and at what menu price. They also differ in "who will direct the efforts of the foodservice manager."

The four basic fields are reviewed in depth and each field's unique set of foodservice requirements and circumstances is evaluated on the following pages; they are:
1. Plants and factories in rural and urban areas
2. Office buildings, primarily in urban areas
3. Schools and colleges
4. Hospitals and institutions

Plants and Factories

Today, American manufacturing operations run the gamut from an automated plant with a few employees up to the gigantic assembly lines with thousands of employees. As employees of these plants are from varied groups, the foodservice requirements also vary. They include cafeterias for "white collar" workers; cafeterias for "blue collar" workers; separate eating areas in the cafeteria for foremen, supervisors or other management personnel; executive foodservice, guest dining rooms, separate president or "board" dining services and vending foodservices.

Some plants are so large and complex that they contain examples of all the groups mentioned, others are so small that they have "vending" only or a simple cafeteria where everyone eats in a "democratic" manner.

Pricing policy for menus is dictated by a variety of criteria. At some companies, the trade union that dominates the plant workers has a "say" in the pricing policy of the foodservice. This is often expressed at the bargaining table and made part of the labor agreement. In other cases, management's paternal attitude toward its workers provides heavy subsidies to the foodservice as an employee benefit, with correspondingly low menu prices. In still other cases, pricing policy is left to a contracted caterer who pays commissions to the plant management or to an employee welfare group. In this situation, prices are comparable to those charged for similar menu items in a public restaurant.

Management personnel are often provided low cost executive dining rooms as part of a management benefit, while "top" management dining rooms are often subsidized 100% as part of their benefits package.

In most large plants, vending services are a source of commission revenue, which is often used to offset foodservice or operator's costs. By the very nature of its cost structure, the vending portion of a plant foodservice has a high profit potential. These profits are a main source of subsidy for plant foodservice operators. (A later chapter on Foodservice Vending will deal with this in greater depth.)

Large Office Buildings

The multi-story office buildings of today's metropolitan areas are often occupied by a single "main tenant" whose name is given to the building. Many of these buildings contain a variety of foodservices, some public and some private.

Street level locations in these buildings often have a coffee shop and "quality" restaurant combination managed by a single or chain operator and operating out of a central kitchen. The practice of establishing multiple "theme" units from one central production source has become common.

Upper floor tenants, particularly the tenant occupying a majority of the building space, often provide executive and employee foodservices at various rates of subsidy. These services are usually an employee cafeteria, coffee cart service and some form of executive dining facility.

The employee cafeteria may serve lunch only or also be open for breakfast. The coffee cart service can be for morning service only or twice daily with an afternoon run also scheduled. Executive dining facilities range from a complete dining room service for specific categories of executive personnel to small dining facilities for a select handful of top management people. Guest dining facilities for use of executives and other business guests are usually combined with executive dining services.

Some companies provide a "service dining room" for all employees at somewhat higher than cafeteria prices but somewhat lower than "street" prices.

Pricing policies are as varied as companies. Insurance companies and banks are noted for low wages and high employee benefits and consider the employee foodservice as a benefit. As a result, meals are often priced at "food cost" and, in some cases, are served free.

The majority of companies endeavor to recover "direct operating costs" and subsidize the capital investment, space and utilities cost and cost of caterer management if the facility is "contracted."

Very few industrial foodservice facilities in office buildings are completely self-sustaining on a regular profit and loss basis. These operations usually find it impossible to pay the landlord a "going rent" for the space used.

Schools and Colleges

This segment of industrial foodservice operation provides service primarily to prep schools and colleges. Although gigantic "school meal systems" exist in the various public school systems, they are usually operated by the municipality and receive some form of government subsidy. Recent changes in Federal laws are opening public schools to industrial caterers but the results are too new to be of value at this time.

Private prep schools are the minor portion of this group and service is for the student and faculty. Style of service is usually "family style" with members of the faculty at each table, often with their wives and children. Students act as waiters and often work as dishwashers as part of assigned duties. Since private schools do not receive government subsidy, meal cost budgets are as high or low as the tuition plan of the school allows.

The major portion of this segment of the industrial food management field is made up of the nation's colleges and universities. These provide various forms of foodservice for students, faculty, administration and guests. Different styles now prevalent include the student cafeteria, student snack bar, faculty dining room, dean's or president's dining room, fraternity dining facilities.

Cafeterias are usually priced moderately for the day students with a package plan of a pre-set price for a full week's meals for the resident student. Snack bars are usually priced to make a profit. Faculty and administration facilities are almost always priced at a "bargain rate," with the president's or dean's foodservice facility often fully paid for by the college. Guest service for visiting parents, provided by the foodservice departments for parents' days, graduations and other special events is usually priced to recover all costs.

Fraternity dining services are usually operated by each fraternity individually in a manner similar to prep school service but without the presence of faculty "chaperones."

College foodservices are operated by professional catering companies or by the college itself, depending on the decisions of the governing body. Some have a heritage of being college-operated while others have never been operated by the institution. These days, the student body or student government has a great voice in this decision, especially in selecting a caterer where one is utilized to manage the foodservice.

Hospitals and Other Institutions

This segment of the industry covers nursing homes, hospitals, mental institutions and other forms of mass housing for the sick or aged.

In the past, professional management of these facilities by "foodservice managers" has been conspicuous by its absence. The A. D. A. dietitian dominated this field of industrial foodservice management until recent years. Recently, the constantly rising cost of the dietary department of the hospital has brought the professional foodservice manager to this field and the dietitian is more often concentrating on supervising the "therapeutic diet" portion of the foodservice. Smaller hospitals have begun to employ the chef/manager where one is available.

Foodservice in this area is always a tray service to the patient from a central or decentralized facility. In addition, a cafeteria or dining facility is provided for the employees, sometimes shared by the medical staff although sometimes there is a separate cafeteria for that group. Top management may or may not have a separate facility for its own service needs.

A coffee shop for visitors is found in most medium-sized and large facilities. This is almost always a profit-making venture, and, as often as not, is operated by an "auxiliary group" who use their profits for philanthropic work in the hospital.

Special function catering is an important part of hospital foodservice management. Board meetings, fund-raising affairs, employee functions and other similar catered affairs are a part of the total package.

Who Do You Work For?

As a chef/manager, or the manager, of an industrial foodservice operation in any of the four categories, the question of "who do you work for?" has many answers. Since the person responsible for the direction of the industrial foodservice manager's efforts also provides the management guidance and controls his advancement and remuneration, this question is of great importance.

There are two basic answers to this question. The first answer applies to the "company" operated facility; there you would work for the designated representative or head of the department of the company, school or institution that is responsible for the operation of the foodservice. The individual designated can and does vary widely from operation to operation, as the following paragraphs make clear.

Business and Industry

Grouping office buildings and plants and factories under the general heading of Business and Industry, responsibility for the foodservice in a caterer-operated facility may fall under any one of the following categories depending on the structure of the company:

1. Industrial Relations Department
2. Personnel Department
3. Office Services Department
4. Real Estate Division
5. Employee Services Division
6. Plant Services Division
7. "Special Assistant" to _____

In all cases, the person delegated by the company to be responsible for the foodservice operation is unlikely to have had a background in the foodservice field. The foodservice manager, if he is to be successful, in addition to being a competent foodservice manager, must also know and understand the philosophies, policies and management goals of the company for whom he is managing the foodservice.

Colleges and Universities

Here again, the foodservice manager may report to the head of a service department or a specifically assigned person. However, more and more often the business manager of the college is being assigned the responsibility for the operation of the college's foodservice. Just as the professional manager is becoming a part of industry, the business manager is the professional manager of the "education industry." While he is not usually well versed in foodservice, his general approach to business has sufficient common sense to make him a practical person to work for.

Hospitals and Other Institutions

The business manager of the educational institution has his counterpart in the Hospital Administrator of this field. Hospital Administration is a complete field of study with its own educational requirements and academic degrees, including the Ph. D. The modern hospital administrator, in an increasing number of cases, is a skilled businessman in the "service" portion of the hospital industry. His functions include the dietary department, housekeeping, laundry and the numerous other services present in a "hotel for sick people," which is what a hospital is. In the larger institutions, an administrator may have several assistants, each assigned a portion of the various services (including dietary) as his sphere of responsibility.

In this area of industrial foodservice management, the manager usually is guided by individuals who have a greater degree of understanding of their institution's foodservice problems rather than those involved in the operation of the institution (i. e. doctors, nurses, etc.) whose concern is not in the foodservice area.

Caterer Operated Facilities

In a "caterer" operated facility, the foodservice is "contracted out" by the company, school or institution to one of the various foodservice organizations that specialize in the management of industrial foodservice operations of all kinds. These companies may also own and operate commercial restaurants, fast food chains, hotels and motels and other segments of the foodservice/lodging industry; this is the case with all of the larger companies.

Should you work for one of these companies, the question of "who do you work for?" has a second answer. The same delegated department head or representative of the "client" organization, as described above, relates to the foodservice operations but under these circumstances his contact is through the representative of the catering company. As a unit chef/manager or manager, you would officially work for the representative of the catering company but be subject to indirect pressures by the representative of the client. In effect, a manager under these circumstances, has the difficult position of "working for two bosses." While his income and potential for advancement is governed by the catering company which is his employer, he must also be successful in satisfying the client's needs and relating to the client representative.

A thorough knowledge of the organizational structure of his own company is essential to the success of the chef/manager or manager. Without this knowledge, he cannot obtain the necessary staff service assistance when required, or plan his own efforts for personal advancement within the company.

The Industrial Caterer

The unit manager or chef/manager usually reports "up" to a district foodservice manager who in turn reports to a regional manager and on up to a division vice president.

The district manager is usually responsible for up to ten individual locations.

The regional manager is usually responsible for more than one district manager plus one or more vending branches (see Chapter IV, Foodservice Vending.) As a regional manager, the employee must be thoroughly knowledgeable about both manual and vending operations. Where a corporation has separate college or hospital divisions, these are usually subdivided into regions, districts and units in the same manner; however, vending is not usually part of the organizational structure. Where a vending responsibility exists in these specialized divisions, it is either made a part of the unit manager's responsibility or is "subbed out" to a branch of the company or even to an outside company.

The two organization charts shown on this page depict (1) the corporate structure and its specialized divisions and (2) a single operating division with its subdivisions of regions and districts.

Companies organized in this manner also profide staff services at the division level; these might include dietitians, executive chefs and food "specialists." These positions are occupied by personnel who are specialists in particular areas and their services are made available to the various units by the different levels of management.

There are many methods of organizing the efforts of management but most of the major companies follow this basic pattern.

Fig. 1–GENERAL MANAGEMENT SUPPORTING STAFF SERVICES

BUSINESS & INDUSTRY DIVISION	HOSPITAL DIVISION	SCHOOL DIVISION
Regions	Regions	Regions
Branches & Districts	Districts	Districts
Units	Units	Units

Fig. 2– SINGLE OPERATING DIVISION

DIVISION VICE PRESIDENT
REGIONAL DIRECTORS

VARIOUS FOOD DISTRICT MANAGERS	VARIOUS VENDING BRANCH MANAGERS
VARIOUS INDIVIDUAL LOCATIONS	VARIOUS VENDING ROUTES & SUPERVISORS

On the whole, the industrial foodservice manager needs astute business ability coupled with a knowledge of advanced management techniques and, in addition, culinary skills, if he is to succeed. Culinary skills alone are not enough. Unless these skills can be related to the specific service goal and management philosophy of the group served, a chef/manager or manager might well fail as an individual even though he is operating an efficient facility. The true measure of efficiency is the manager's ability to coordinate his department into the overall organization which his department services. Unlike a commercial foodservice venture, the industrial foodservice manager is not judged by the profit picture alone but by his ability to meet the *cost and service* goals of his employer and/or client.

Entry Jobs to Industrial Foodservice Management

For the person desiring to enter the field of industrial foodservice management, there are various entry jobs, especially for one skilled in the culinary arts.

Manager's positions in industrial foodservice are of two types:
>   The administrative manager
>   The chef-manager

The administrative manager is used in a facility that can afford both a chef and a manager. The person in that position can (1) come up "through the ranks," as in any field of endeavor, (2) gain his position through educational effort in the two- or four-year college or (3) advance from the position of chef/manager of a smaller unit.

The primary entry position for one with culinary skills is as a chef/manager of a smaller location. Such facilities usually employ 20 or fewer foodservice workers and cannot afford both a chef and a manager, so the position is combined. Employment is available from both company-operated and caterer-operated facilities. Employment as a chef/manager for a company-operated facility can be a dead-end street for the young manager looking for a career in foodservice, as his employer is not primarily in the foodservice business. The same position with an industrial catering company can be a springboard to a successful career in food production, food management or various other areas of the food field.

Advancement is available in various ways to the chef/manager employed by a food management company:

a) *Advancement to an administrative management position in a larger unit*— Here he can utilize his culinary skills and management knowledge to direct the staff much more effectively than the administrative manager who does not possess culinary skills.

b) *Advancement to Executive Chef*—Here his culinary skills are utilized by his employer to open new units; improve the food production ability of chefs and/or chef/managers with lesser skills; supervise food preparation in multi-units for special occasions and similar responsibilities. This position is comparable to that of an Executive Chef of a hotel but on a multi-unit basis rather than within one facility.

c) *Advancement to upper management positions*—Through either of the efforts described above, by first learning the basics and then making advanced use of management knowledge and techniques, the chef/manager can advance to the top level executive positions of any company.

Modern trends toward pre-fabricated and convenience foods have allowed many men to be successful in the field of industrial food management without a base of culinary knowledge. While culinary skills are no longer required to be a successful manager, they are a tremendous plus factor when you possess them.

III: The Operating Goal

A good management plan has as its sole purpose the attainment of a desired objective. That being the case, a clear definition of the objective is a must for proper management planning. Industrial foodservice management is no exception and has the same prerequisite for management planning: a clear statement of the objective of the foodservice.

Unlike a commercial restaurant whose sole purpose is to produce profit for its owner, an industrial foodservice exists to increase the productivity of its customers, in one way or another.

While the operating policy of a restaurant is controlled by its owner, "policy," in the form of goals, for an industrial foodservice is dictated by the company providing the service. The catering company's goals will prevail rather than the usual foodservice goal of "a profit from the sale of prepared foods." In industrial cafeterias, foodservice is just one part of an overall management goal and the industrial foodservice manager is often left out when service policy for the area of his responsibility is being established. To be successful, the industrial foodservice manager must be able to gain the necessary recognition from management so he will be allowed to participate when "policy" regarding the foodservice is being reviewed or established.

Establishing the Objective

All industrial foodservices have two distinct aspects that are always considered in defining their operating goal.

1. Financial Limitations (money)
2. Service Requirements (need)

While their specific definition will vary as it is applied to the four main fields of industrial foodservice, these two basic aspects will always be considered when the operating goal (objective) of any industrial foodservice operation is set.

Let's look at four examples of objectives, defined as operating goals, as they may be applied to 1) plants and factories; 2) office buildings; 3) schools and colleges and 4) hospitals.

Example One—Office Building

A corporation occupying the major portion of a midtown office building with 2,000 employees at all levels may establish its operating goal as:

1.   To provide an employee cafeteria to serve lunch within a 60-minute period to 2,000 people released, one-fourth at a time, at 20-minute intervals; menu prices to be 25% lower than nearby commercial foodservice establishments.

And

2.   To provide morning and afternoon coffee cart service at competitive prices to all employees within a one-hour period starting at 9 a. m. and at 2:30 p. m.

And

3.   To provide executive dining facilities for 100 executives daily and an additional 30-40 executive guests daily in a "quality" fashion plus filling special catering requirements for board of directors lunches, sales meetings, etc., with the total cost of this service to be borne by the company.

Example Two—Manufacturing Plant

A large manufacturing plant employing a total of 4,000 workers on three shifts, operating six days per week, may establish its goal as follows:

1.   To provide separate cafeterias for white collar and blue collar workers serving white collar workers five days per week first shift and serving blue collar workers three shifts, six days per week. Menu price structures to be part of union agreement and price increases not allowed without prior union approval; however, management does not wish to subsidize the cafeterias.

And

2.   Provide executive dining facilities for middle management in a "service dining room." Management will subsidize the cost of all extra labor required.

And

3.   Provide top management with all daily and special service requirements, completely subsidized by the company.

And

4.   Utilize vending machines at strategic locations for all "break periods" in order to keep shop personnel as near their work assembly stations as possible. Vending prices may be comparable to commercial competition and normal vending commissions may be used to offset part of the cost of cafeteria operations.

Example Three—College

A college on a campus may establish its operating goal as:

1.   To provide cafeteria meal service to all "boarding" students for 20 meals per week at a $14.00 per student rate. The boarding rate must cover food, labor and direct expenses and the caterer's profit, where a caterer is used, with the college providing the facility, utilities and replacements. Also to provide an a la carte menu for day students at menu prices

comparable to the weekly meal plan prices charged to boarding students.

And

2. To provide "snack bar" service during after-school hours for all students, faculty and campus visitors, with beer available on weekend evenings. Profits, if any, from this facility to be used to offset the operating costs of the student cafeteria and faculty dining room service.

And

3. Provide a faculty dining area adjacent to the cafeteria for table service to the faculty, menu prices to be the same as the day student cafeteria level.

Example Four—Hospital

A voluntary hospital or institution may establish an operating goal as:
1. Provide foodservice to patients at a cost not to exceed $5.00 per patient day for food, labor and supplies, plus the caterer's profit where a caterer is used.

And

2. Provide foodservice to employees in a cafeteria with a menu price structure geared to recover the cost of food, labor and supplies.

And

3. Provide coffee shop service, geared to make a profit, to visitors; profit to be used by the Ladies Auxiliary of the hospital for philanthropic purposes within the hospital.

In each of these four examples, a clear statement of the foodservice needs and financial goals has been formulated. Unfortunately, the chef/manager or manager will not always find these conditions clearly stated at his assigned unit. It is of real importance to the manager's success and the success of his operation for him to be able to define his own department objectives and get his own management to recognize and accept his definitions. A good industrial foodservice manager is one who can "push" the decision makers and so make sure of an operating goal that can be clearly defined, since it is by this goal that his own performance can be measured and his future wage increases and advancement guaranteed.

The Operating Budget

An excellent method of assuring supervisory participation in establishing the operating goal is to prepare and present an annual budget to management. This document should clearly outline both the financial and service requirements for the coming year. Every facility, whether it is a hospital, school, plant or office, prepares an annual budget. The budget the unit manager prepares should be similar to the following basic outline, with variations as may be required for special circumstances:

1.   **Plant or Office Building–Business, Industry**

   A.   Statement of service requirements as you understand or recommend them to be.
   B.   Estimate of sales income expected.
   C.   Estimate of food cost ratio to sales.
   D.   Estimate of payroll expenditures with detail of number of people and man/hours required to meet service needs.
   E.   Evaluation of payroll related costs.
   F.   Estimate of other direct operating costs for:
      1. Paper Goods and Supplies
      2. Laundry
      3. Cleaning Supplies
      4. Repair and Replacement
      5. Insurance
      6. Misc.–Other Costs
   G.   Total of all estimated costs and sales summarized into an estimated annual operating statement similar to the format on facing page.

This projected statement, together with detailed back-up information for all areas of sales and costs, clearly establishes the financial and service goals of the operation and, after presentation, will require a decision by top management. This decision is sometimes difficult to obtain. The decision makers almost always become experts when analyzing the food-service budget, although they usually do not have food management experience. They can and will suggest various ways and means to *increase* service and *reduce* costs that are quite impossible.

The capable manager must have all his facts at hand to back up his budget presentation in order to win his case. It is on presentation of the budget that the operating goal of the location is established and defined. An office building budget format is shown in Fig. 3, facing page.

2.   **Hospital and/or Other Institution**

Hospitals, nursing homes and other similar institutions follow an accounting procedure that differs greatly from the plant or office building. Presentation of a budget for an institution of this type should conform fairly closely to the following format:
   A.   Statement of service requirements for patients, employees, professional staff and visitors. If the hospital has a service policy, restate it. If a service policy does not exist, state what you believe to be the necessary policy to achieve proper operations.
   B.   Estimate of patient days expected in the coming year.
   C.   Estimate of food cost per patient day.
   D.   Estimate of gross labor cost evaluated on a per patient day basis.
   E.   Estimate of supplies cost per patient day.
   F.   A summarized gross cost per patient day for food, labor and supplies.

If a "pay" employee cafeteria is part of the service, for budget purposes sales income from the cafeteria should be credited against food purchases. Coffee shop sales and costs, if any, are always kept completely separate.

A hospital budget format is presented in Fig. 4, p. 18.

Fig. 3 – BUDGET FORMAT – OFFICE BUILDING CORPORATION

1. Sales

        Cafeteria $_____

        Coffee carts $_____

        Executive and guest dining $_____

                                Total Sales $_____   100%

II. Food Cost $_____   ____%

III. Payroll $_____

        Payroll related costs $_____

                               Total Labor Cost $_____   ____%

IV. Direct Expenses

        Paper goods $_____

        Cleaning supplies $_____

        Laundry $_____

        Replacements $_____

        Insurance $_____

        Misc. other costs $_____

                      Total Direct Expenses $_____   ____%

V. Total All Costs $_____   ____%

VI. Net Profit (or Loss) $_____   ____%

Fig. 4–XYZ HOSPITAL BUDGET FORMAT

Estimated annual patient days		_____
Gross Food Purchases	$_____	
Less Cafeteria Cash Income	$_____	
Net Food Cost	$_____	
Food Cost Per Patient Day		$_____
Estimated Labor Cost	$_____	
Payroll Related Costs	$_____	
Sub Total	$_____	
Labor Cost Per Patient Day		$_____
Supplies Cost	$_____	
Supplies Cost Per Patient Day		$_____
Total Dietary Cost		$_____
Dietary Cost Per Patient Day		$_____

Back-up information for the budget consisting of specific menus, menu cycles, labor schedules, union contracts where existing and similar information must all be available. In some cases, where the possibility of a wide variance in annual patient/days can be expected, sliding scale schedules of variations in the expected cost per patient day should be presented. Hospital dietary department costs are part of overall hospital costs, reimbursed in part to the hospital by Blue Cross, Medicaid, Medicare and other similar agencies. The hospital administrator has become increasingly cognizant of the effect of proper dietary department budgeting and cost accounting to assure his institution proper and timely reimbursement for that service. As manager, your ability to coordinate the dietary budget plan to the hospital budget plan can assure the establishment of a clearly defined operating goal.

3. Schools and Colleges

Budgeting the school or college combines some of the elements of the Business and Industry technique with some of the Hospital technique. Sales and costs from the a la carte menu, the faculty dining service, the snack bar, etc. are projected similar to the methods used for Business and Industry operations. Sales and costs of the boarding students cafeteria are projected similar to the hospital "patient/day," only now they are called "student meals." A basic pattern for a budget could look like this:

A.   Statement of services required for students, employees, faculty, guests and special occasions.

B.   Projection of numbers of boarding students expected; boarding students are usually referred to as "contracts."

C.   Projection of number of meals to be provided per contract.

D.   Projection of food cost per contract.

E.   Estimate of sales from other sources (day students, snack bar, etc.)

F.   Projection of labor costs.

G.   Projection of all other costs.

H.   A summarized annual statement covering the above.

Fig. 5–SCHOOL OR COLLEGE BUDGET STATEMENT

Sales

Contracts		$_____
Cash Sales		$_____
	Total Sales	$_____

Food Cost

Contracts		$_____
Cash Sales		$_____
	Total Food Cost	$_____

Payroll Related Costs		$_____
All Other Costs (Direct Expenses)		$_____
	Total Cost	$_____
	Net Profit or Loss	$_____

Separate summaries "breaking out" or covering special areas should be included as supporting material. Many variations can be made in this presentation depending on the individual circumstances. However, this format can be used as a starting point for planning.

General Budgeting

A later chapter on budgeting goes into this subject in greater depth and detail, giving examples of sales projections and costs as part of the case histories included in that chapter.

Profit or Productivity–Objective of the Manager

The question is often asked, "Where does the profit come from in an industrial foodservice?" It is also often asked, "What is the difference between operating an industrial foodservice and a commercial restaurant?" The "profit" is known as "productivity" and the difference is in the "objective."

A commercial restaurant and an industrial foodservice have much in common as foodservice facilities. Both types of operations have the management problems of buying food, hiring people, serving the customer, and the related work of sanitation, maintenance, etc. But the difference in their goals accounts for considerable difference in the management effort required. While the commercial restaurant exists solely to make a monetary profit for its owner, the industrial foodservice operation exists primarily to service the company's employee needs, often defined as increased productivity. When the goal is employee productivity, the motivation and objective of the foodservice manager differ from those of the manager who needs to make a profit.

A comparison of the motivations of two operating managers, one working in a commercial enterprise and the other in an industrial foodservice, can aid a new unit manager in developing his personal philosophy about establishing his operating goal. The following comparison should be helpful.

The Commercial (Restaurant) Operation

A commercial enterprise has as its sole operating goal a satisfactory return on investment; this is called profit. The only measure of success for a commercial foodservice is the percentage of profit related to sales and investment. The manager of this type of business has complete authority over the regulation of his business hours, menu format and prices, style and type of service and all other facets of his business. Restricted solely by his own ability to provide the money, either from sales and profits or on credit, he may make additional capital investment as he deems desirable. While his operation performs a community service of a type, that service is performed only as a means toward making a profit. If for any reason the operator closes his restaurant, others will absorb his customers and provide the community with the same service.

The Industrial Foodservice

In an industrial foodservice, profit is measured in various ways which can be given the common denominator of increased productivity. All operating costs must be met, with a profit to the contract caterer when one is used, but these costs are not usually covered solely by the income from sales. In almost every case, some form of subsidy is required.

Management provides this subsidy because (1) it feels that the foodservice adds to its employees' productivity; (2) it is forced to do so by conditions or as part of a labor/management agreement. In any case, foodservice is not the main business of the employer.

Increased productivity, via a good foodservice that assures employee contentment, is an intangible item. There is no way to prove or disprove the effect on the production of an individual of the morale factor, although this can be heavily influenced by the foodservice. The phrase, "An army travels on its stomach" is an old saying which can be applied to many areas. Some of the definitions of profit through increased productivity used to enforce the theory are as follows:

1.   An employee of a manufacturing plant or office building, contented with his surroundings and services (including the foodservice), is more likely to work to maximum capacity, thereby increasing overall productivity and eventually effecting higher profits.

2.   A student, contented with his surroundings, learns at the rate of his maximum potential, so increasing his productivity. This eventually is of profit to himself and his community.

3.   A patient who is well fed and happy gets well faster and he personally profits. In each of these definitions, profit has been portrayed as eventual through "productivity" or personal contentment.

The manager who establishes the operating goal of an industrial foodservice defines the specific profit and method of achieving it for his operating unit. As stated at the beginning of this chapter, a good management plan has as its sole purpose attainment of a desired objective. The ability to clearly define that objective, primarily in terms of financial and service goals and, secondarily, with an understanding of profit vs. productivity, is paramount to an industrial foodservice manager's success.

IV: Understanding and Applying Management Principles

There are many definitions of the word, "management." From the simple phrase:
"Management is accomplishment"
to the more comprehensive explanation:
"Management is the achieving of objectives through effective use of available resources."
"Management" is defined in a variety of ways.

It would be impossible to provide a comprehensive course on management within the confines of this book and it will not be attempted. What will be presented in this chapter are some generalities on the application of modern management techniques as they apply to industrial foodservice operation. The student desiring to delve deeper into the basic field of management should do so through independent study. A few recommended books are listed at the end of this chapter, p.25. Many successful businessmen feel that management is the base from which all business success is derived, and that could well be so.

Many foodservice managers think that foodservice is a "tough" business and that people in other business "don't understand our problems." While this may be true about the specific problems of foodservice, it is not true about its degree of "toughness." Other "service" businesses, and most retail businesses, are just as complex in their operations as the foodservice business. Success in any field of endeavor is the result of sound planning and the application of good management methods to that planning. It has been wisely said, "Commitment is half the battle. The first and most important half."

There is absolutely no difference in the management approach required by the foodservice industry and that required by any other industry. The key is the words "management approach." In the business world the executive with the true management approach "makes" things happen, he doesn't "let" things happen. True success is rarely accidental, it is usually planned, either formally or informally.

Developing a Management Philosophy

The modern manager who is successful in any field has developed a management philosophy that combines common sense with the specific knowledge about his industry that is necessary to achieve the end result desired. Effort expended must be put forth with the desired goal kept constantly in mind. We are all familiar with the unorganized type of cook who works himself to death turning out a small meal while with less effort the expert chef turns out a large, magnificent meal and makes it look easy. Whether he describes it as such or not, the expert has a management philosophy that lets him make things happen according to plan.

Each new industrial foodservice manager must establish his own management philosophy as to how he will make things happen. While one man's philosophy may differ in detail from another's, the basics are always the same.

"The basic function of a manager is to make things happen."

"The basic function of a foodservice manager is to make a successful foodservice happen." How to do it is encompassed in a simplified management method: PLAN, ORGANIZE AND ACT to meet an objective.

Step one in the system is to firmly establish the objective. This was discussed in detail in Chapter III. Knowing who will be served what—where and when—and at what menu selling price is the core of the objective.

Industrial organizations have what is referred to as "company policy" in many areas of personnel, operations, etc. A policy *must* also be set for the foodservice operation but more often it is not. If there isn't a "policy," the unit manager must be sure that one is established. It is a mistake to allow a vacuum to exist; if a policy vacuum is encountered, be sure to fill it or something (or someone) else will.

Once the policy or objective is clearly established, the manager is ready to take step one of PLAN, ORGANIZE AND ACT.

How to Plan

Planning is considered the most important step in management. The essence of good planning is the correct use of the "5 M's" of management planning:

1. *Men*
2. *Money*
3. *Materials*
4. *Methods*
5. *Machines*

Whether it is a foodservice or a factory, a complete and efficient plan makes the best use of all of the 5 M's. Remember—the plan must be rooted in the objective. If there is anything in the plan that is not required to meet the objective, it is unnecessary. Let's take the five M's, one at a time, and look at them in detail.

1.   *Men*—This covers the man/hours available to you. The number of employees allotted multiplied by the number of hours they work each day equals man/hours per day. These man/hours are your most valued resource in producing your food, serving your customers, cleaning your facility and for all the rest of the work you, as manager, are responsible for. You must plan who is supposed to do what and when, in detail. To do this you must prepare:

a)   Detailed job descriptions defining the duties of each category of employee.
b)   Detailed job breakdowns defining the work of each individual employee.

c)   Clear-cut work schedules.

d)   Clear-cut assignment of individual responsibility.

The good manager plans the effective use of his man/hours and then correctly directs and supervises them to see that they are effective.

2.   *Money*—Money is your working capital. Whether it comes as cash flow from your customer via the register sale or as subsidy from your company to overcome an operating loss, it is not unlimited. Large corporations plan their cash flow with the help of special finance officers whose job it is to assure that the company always has sufficient working capital when necessary and a satisfactory cash reserve or credit at all times.

The successful plan includes the forecasting of money requirements and determining where the needed money will come from. Timely processing of bills to assure maximum discounts is the same as making a cash sale. This is one example of "money planning." Your money plan must include every area of money received, spent or handled.

3.   *Material*—In our business, the primary material is food. Plans must be established to assure that it is ordered, received, stored and processed in a controlled manner. Food is a "soft" product and can be easily "lost" while it is in inventory. While a can of beans today is a can of beans tomorrow, the same does not hold true for a piece of pastry, a tomato or any other highly perishable part of our "materials." Materials require complete planning for their use in our business.

Secondarily, our materials consist of cleaning supplies, laundry and other similar items. While these are not perishable, they can be used in excess and are easily wasted. All of these materials must be given consideration in your materials planning.

4.   *Methods*—Methods are the means by which our products are prepared and made ready for sale. A recipe is a method; a menu is a method; an inventory system is a method; all existing for the sole purpose of providing the product to be sold.....FOOD.

Standard operating methods and procedures must be established for every phase of work. A "standard" is the result achieved when a satisfactory job is performed. Standards can be achieved through planning the use of correct methods.

5.   *Machines*—These are the tools that assist man to be more productive. In our business, machines are stoves, refrigerators, cash registers, toasters, coffee urns and similar pieces of equipment. Machines represent a capital investment and the use of the operation's money. They absorb the effect of your man/hours as they are operated and cleaned. Each machine must produce its share of the work effort, otherwise the capital invested and the man/hours expended in its use will be wasted.

A manager's planning must include proper scheduling of machine use; planning a properly balanced menu insures the best use of oven, top of stove, fryer and steamer, whereas a lopsided menu will burden one piece of equipment while another stands idle.

Your plan must also include proper cleaning and maintenance schedules to protect the life expectancy of the equipment. Most companies maintain a capital investment program under which equipment is depreciated over a period of years. Your plan must assure that your machines will last the lifetime of their depreciation.

All five—*Men, Money, Materials, Methods, Machines*—must be coordinated into a single plan geared to meet *your* objective as the manager. Your plan must be reviewed periodically, at least annually, to assure that it is still effective. Remember, plan only to meet the objective that has been set for your operation; *do not overplan.*

How to Organize

After your plan is complete, organize it for action. Remember, your plan of "organization" must be designed for the same reason that you prepared the basic plan: to effectively achieve the objective.

Organization puts structure into a plan. It is the skeleton, the framework, that holds a plan together. When you go to the bank to make a deposit, the bank has *you* fill out a slip with all the necessary information on it for *their* use. That is organization on the bank's part; all they do is take your money; you have done their work.

Any act of administration that is repeated can be organized with some sort of a form. In today's computer age, many things can be organized via the computer. The accounting and banking functions of most businesses are now computerized as part of their organizational effort.

To the industrial foodservice operator, organization means planned forms for administrative control of the various facets of operation. These should be geared to suit your own specific needs without requiring repetition of any actions on your part. Finally, *be sure the organization fits the plan.*

Now—To Act

The key ingredient to the picture is *you*, the foodservice manager. It is you who must take your plan, through your organization of menus, forms, systems and other methods, and *make it happen.* To do this, you must supervise yourself and follow through. It is you, the manager, who is the leader of the work gang. You as leader set the pace and if you are a good leader, your subordinates will follow you.

There is a saying:
"If you have the quality of leadership—cherish it. If not—cultivate it." That's a must for any manager.

Don't forget—the basic function of a foodservice manager is to make a foodservice happen. Establish a clearly defined objective. *P-O-A* to meet your objective and watch things happen.

RECOMMENDED READINGS ON MANAGEMENT

Appley, Lawrence A. *Values in Management.* New York: American Management Association, 1968.

Coffman, James P. *The High Payroll, Low Profit Syndrome.* Boston: Institutions/Cahners, 1970.

Drucker, Peter F. *The Practice of Management.* New York: Harper & Row, 1954.

Dyer, Dewey A. *So You Want to Start a Restaurant.* Boston: Institutions/Cahners, 1971.

Gellerman, Saul W. *Management by Motivation and Productivity.* New York: American Management Association, 1963.

Heyel, Carl. *Organizing Your Job in Management.* New York: Macmillan, 1960.

Merrill, Harwood F. ed. *Classics in Management.* New York: American Management Association, 1970.

Stokes, John W. *How To Manage a Restaurant or Institutional Foodservice.* Dubuque, Iowa: Wm. C. Brown Publishers, 1967.

West, Bessie Brooks and Levelle Wood. *Food Service in Institutions,* 3rd ed. New York: John Wiley & Sons, Inc. 1955.

V: The Operating Budget

Perhaps the most important planning job performed by a unit manager is the annual preparation of the operating budget. It is at this time that a manager has the opportunity to re-establish the unit's operating objective and obtain top management's approval of it. Chapter III outlined basic budget preparation formats; these will be dealt with in greater detail in this chapter.

The Budget Format

There is no standard budget format that will suffice for all situations. Each location and company has individual needs. There is, however a good standard definition to follow in establishing a format for budget presentation:

The budget format should follow the exact pattern of the monthly accounting statement.

If the management of your company uses a specific format in preparing the accounting statements each month, all levels of management are accustomed to reading and understanding the "language of accounting." If you prepare and present your budget in the "language" that is spoken in your business environment, you have the best chance possible to be heard and understood.

Every company, school or hospital foodservice should be operated as a separate efficient business. Whether it be a "profit and loss" facility, subsidized or management-fee, caterer or company operated, the foodservice of a company or an institution is a separate business. The need to assess sales or income, operating costs and net profit or loss requires detailed study but such study does not have to be restricted to the professional business manager or cost accountant.

The foodservice manager surely knows more about his area of operation than any other person on the management team. By simply preparing a review of his financial condition as precisely as he would prepare a recipe for a favorite dish, budget preparation can be easily accomplished by any industrial foodservice operator.

Let's take a few case histories and prepare four operating budgets; these will be for an office building, plant, hospital and school/college.

CASE HISTORY NO. 1–URBAN OFFICE BUILDING

Chapter III cited an office building with a population of 2,000 people that has an employee cafeteria, twice-daily coffee cart service and an executive/guest dining facility. For the accounting format for preparing the monthly statement for this operation, see Fig. 5A, page 28.

In preparing the budget for this operation, it is necessary to evaluate and explain expected sales and costs on each line of the operating statement. The statement is categorized into:

I. Sales   III. Payroll Cost
II. Food Cost   IV. Direct Expenses

Your budget presentation should follow the same categories. The budget presentation should also contain a statement of policy as it is understood to exist and/or recommendations for changes in policy.

Index of Budget

The index of your budget should look like this:
I.   Introduction–statement of policy
II.   Sales projection
III. Food cost projection
IV.   Labor cost projection and man/hours survey
V.   Payroll related costs
VI.   Direct operating expenses
VII. Summary
VIII. Recommendations

Note that this method of presentation allows the manager to begin by summarizing policy as he understands it to exist and ends by allowing him to make recommendations for change when he feels improvements can be made.

Now let's review point by point and prepare the budget:

I. Introduction–Statement of Policy

Presented below is a typical statement that can be made to "set the stage" for budget preparation:

"The following budget projection has been made for the coming fiscal year for the employee foodservice of Office Building Corp.

"Studies and cost projections have been made continuing the present policy of serving breakfast and lunch in the cafeteria, providing a morning and afternoon coffee cart service, using ten carts, and an executive and guest dining service for lunch. Special affairs as required will be catered from the cafeteria. Menu prices will be maintained to reflect a 50% food cost on overall sales mix.

"The present 'on premises' bakery will continue to be operated, and all hot entrees will be freshly prepared in our own kitchen. In general, a high quality of food preparation will be maintained."

Fig 5A–MONTHLY STATEMENT–OFFICE BUILDING CORPORATION

1. Sales

    Cafeteria $_____

    Coffee carts $_____

    Executive and guest dining $_____

                          Total Sales $_____   100%

II. Food Cost $_____   ___%

III. Payroll $_____

     Payroll related costs $_____

                          Total Labor Cost $_____   ___%

IV. Direct Expenses

     Paper goods $_____

     Cleaning supplies $_____

     Laundry $_____

     Replacements $_____

     Insurance $_____

     Misc. other costs $_____

                          Total Direct Expenses $_____   ___%

V. Total All Costs $_____   ___%

VI. Net Profit (or Loss) $_____   ___%

This statement establishes the basic policy as the unit manager and the company understand it. Once the statement of policy is complete, the accounting format assessment begins with a projection of sales.

II. Sales Projection

Sales projections are made by evaluating the number of customers expected at each period of sales and the check average of each customer for each period of sales. In this case, we have the following periods of sales:
1. Breakfast
2. Morning coffee run
3. Lunch
4. Afternoon coffee run
5. Executive and guest dining

Customer count for each period of sales is evaluated as an average daily percentage of the total population. This can be accomplished by a survey of past ratio of customer count related to population figures at that time. Establishing these ratios is important because population figures will fluctuate. As the company increases or decreases its employment, these ratios will serve to show expected increases or decreases in customer counts and resulting sales.

These two figures produce the following formula to evaluate sales:
1. Estimated customer count *multiplied by:*
2. Estimated check average *equals:*
3. Projected sales

Put this all together and prepare a sales projection chart for the 2,000 employees of the Office Building Corporation. It will look like this:

Period	% of Participation	Average Daily Customers	Est.Check Average	Estimated Average Daily Sales
Breakfast	5%	100	40¢	$ 40.
Lunch	65%	1300	70¢	910.
AM Coffee cart	65%	1300	19¢	247.
PM Coffee cart	30%	600	16¢	96.
Exec. and guest dining	75 daily	75	2.00	150.
			Total	$1,443.

X 250 operating days per year = Estimated Annual Sales $360,750.

It should be restated at this point in the budget presentation that the projected sales figure is based on a continuation of the same level of employment, 2,000, and no change in the service policy.

III. Food Cost Projection

The introduction stated that, as a matter of policy, food cost ratio to sales would be 50% and menu price would be adjusted accordingly. This clearly covers that line "II. Food Cost" of your projected statement and will be 50% of all projected sales. In this case $180,375.

IV. Labor Cost Projection

In presenting labor cost projections, it is wise to include a complete survey of positions, number of workers in each position, weekly man/hours worked in each category, present wages, expected cost of increased wages and total estimated annual wages. Such a survey makes it possible for management to have a complete understanding of the manpower required to provide each type of service that they have requested and the cost of that service. An illustration of the estimated labor requirements and costs for this case history is shown in Fig. 7, the summary on the facing page.

V. Payroll Related Costs

Various companies list different cost categories as payroll related costs. These costs are of two types:

1. Those that can be related to payroll as a ratio to the payroll dollar.
2. Those that cost a specific amount per employee per man/hours or per week.

Examples of the first category are:
Unemployment Insurance, State and Federal
Social Security Insurance (F.I.C.A. Tax)
Workmen's Compensation Insurance
Union Welfare Packages
Sick Days Pay
State Disability Insurance

Examples of the second category are:
Accident and Health Insurance
Group Life Insurance
Pension Plan Payments

Some companies may show these categories as payroll related, others may not. The accounting statement format of the Office Building Corporation does, so here is a breakdown of the Payroll Related Costs summary as it might appear in that budget:

Fig. 6—PAYROLL RELATED COSTS

Annual Payroll $141, 635—Total Employees 36

Item	% of Payroll	Cost per Employee	Projected Annual Total Dollar Cost
Social Security	5.1%		$ 7,223
State and Fed. Unemployment Insurance	2.3%		3,257
State Disability Insurance	.4%		566
Workmen's Compensation Insurance	1.5%		2,124
Union Welfare	.3%		424
Accident and Health Insurance		2.00 wk.	3,744
Group Life		3.00 mo.	5,616
Pension Plan	4. %		5,665
		Total	$28,619
		Ratio to Total Payroll	20.2%

VI. Direct Operating Expenses

Direct operating expenses are those incurred directly for the service of the customers. Primarily these are for paper goods, cleaning supplies and laundry. In addition, many companies add the cost of replacements and miscellaneous other minor costs. Contracted-cater-

Fig. 7–MAN/HOURS AND PAYROLL COST SUMMARY

Position	No. of Workers	Total Weekly Man/Hours	Wage Rate	Present Weekly Wage Cost
I. *Supervision and Admin.*				
Manager	1	40	$200 wk.	$200
Asst. Manager	1	40	125 wk.	125
Clerk	1	40	75 wk.	75
Sub Total	3	120		$400
II. *Production*				
Chef	1	40	$175 wk.	$175
Cook	2	80	2.00 hr.	160
Kitchen man	2	70	1.75 hr.	122
Baker	1	40	160 wk.	160
Baker's helper	1	40	2.00 hr.	80
Gen'l. utility	2	70	1.50 hr.	105
Sub Total	9	300		$802
III. *Service*				
Cafeteria supervision	1	40	$110 wk.	$110
Coffee cart/bus workers	10	350	1.50 hr.	525
General service workers	6	210	1.50 hr.	315
Cashiers	2	40	1.75 hr.	70
Sub Total	19	640		$1,020
IV. *Sanitation*				
Head utility	1	40	$ 90 wk.	$ 90
Gen'l. utility	4	140	1.50 hr.	210
Sub Total	5	180		$300

TOTAL RECAPITULATION

I.	3	120		$400
II.	9	300		802
III.	19	640		1,020
IV.	5	180		300
Total	36	1240		$2,522 wk.

52 weeks annual wages		$131,144
8% reserve for wage increases		10,491
Projected annual payroll		$141,635

ing companies usually add the cost of some types of insurance. The Office Building Corporation is a contracted-caterer operation and includes all these costs.

In some cases, an operation may be charged for rent, utilities, depreciations of the capital investment, telephone and various other fixed charges. These must be considered where they exist; however, for the purposes of this case history, they have been omitted. The direct operating expenses might appear in your budget in the following manner:

A. *Paper Goods*
   8% of coffee cart sales of $85,750 $ 6,860
   plus 2% of cafeteria sales of $237, 500   4,750
                                        Total $11,610

B. *Cleaning Supplies*
   An average of 1/2% of gross sales $ 1,803

C. *Laundry*
   An average of $2.50 per week per employee
      ($2.50 x 36 x 52) $ 4,680
   PLUS
   An average of $10 per week for kitchen
      towels and rags $ 520
   PLUS
   An average of 40¢ per customer for table linens
      and napkins in executive dining area
      (.40 x 75 x 250) $ 7,500
                                        Total $12,700

D. *Replacements*
   An average of 2% of gross sales $ 7,212

E. *Insurance*
   An average of 1/2% gross sales $ 1,803

F. *Misc. Other Charges*
   i.e. garbage disposal, office supplies, etc. $ 3,000

                  Total Direct Operating Expenses $55,948

VII. Summary

The summary section of the budget merely recapitulates all the supporting documents in the format of the accounting statement. In the case of the Office Building Corporation of N. Y., this will look like the statement, Fig. 8, facing page. The $28,007 projected operating loss is the amount of the requested budget.

Fig. 8–ANNUAL PROJECTED STATEMENT
OFFICE BUILDING CORPORATION, NEW YORK CITY

I. Sales

    Cafeteria $237,500

    Coffee carts $ 85,750

    Executive and guest dining $ 37,500

                          Total Sales $360,750   100%

II. Food Cost $180,375   50%

III. Payroll $141,635

    Payroll related costs $ 28,619

                  Total Labor Cost $170,254   47.2%

IV. Direct Expenses

    Paper goods $ 11,610

    Cleaning supplies $ 1,803

    Laundry $ 12,700

    Replacements $ 1,803

    Insurance $ 7,212

    Misc. other costs $ 3,000

            Total Direct Expenses $ 38,128   10.6%

V. Total All Costs $388,757   107.8%

VI. Net Profit (or Loss) $ 28,007   (7.8)%

VIII. Recommendations

Most companies would like to operate their employee foodservice at no loss and recover all direct operating expenses from sales. It is prudent for a unit manager to make recommendations that can accomplish that goal. In the case of the Office Building Corporation, a review of the statement shows $30,524 for laundry and $240 per week ($16,000 per year with payroll related costs) to operate a bake shop. Of the $30,524 for laundry, $7,500 is for table linens for the executive dining area. Recommendations would include:

1.   Elimination of the bake shop and purchase of all baked goods; could save two workers.

2.   Replace linen service with a quality place mat and paper napkin service.

3.   Utilize more convenience foods and reduce kitchen labor.

4.   Reduce coffee carts from 10 to 6; would save four workers.

There could be other similar recommendations. In general, this section provides an opportunity for a unit manager to show his initiative and recommend changes and improvements that will require policy changes in operation.

Capital Investment Budget

Almost all operations require some new or additional equipment annually. Almost all companies prepare a *capital equipment* budget annually. The foodservice manager of an industrial foodservice must acquaint himself with the procedure and forms necessary to make his request for capital funds.

It is wise to prepare a list of all capital equipment, its age, its depreciation date, and the expected date of replacement and to keep this information on file for ready reference. Various forms exist in accounting handbooks and manuals for this purpose. The definition of "capital equipment" will vary from company to company. Usually any item costing more than $100 is referred to as capital equipment. You must find out what policy your company has and be sure to prepare an annual "capital" budget accordingly.

CASE HISTORY NO. 2–THE MANUFACTURING PLANT

An industrial plant with 4,000 employees on three shifts operating six days per week, comparable to that shown in Chapter III, would have a budget prepared in a similar manner to the Office Building Corp.; Case History No. 1. We shall call this The Rural Mfg. Co. Some changes would be required in the projection of sales, but all remaining categories would be projected in the same manner.

Sales Projection

A review of Chapter III shows that the RURAL MFG. CO. operates two cafeterias: one for plant workers called the "blue collar cafeteria" and one for office workers called the "white collar cafeteria." They also operate a dining room for foreman-level personnel, called the "service dining room," and an executive dining area. There are no coffee carts and coffee breaks are serviced with vending machines. In order to project sales for this operation, the following breakdowns must be evaluated.

1.   Plant (blue collar) population, by *shift.*

2.   Office (white collar) population.

3.   Number of employees eligible to use the service dining area.

4   Number of executives who will use the executive dining room.

This should result in a sales breakdown format similar to Fig. 9, facing page.

Fig. 9–SALES BREAKDOWN SUMMARY
RURAL MANUFACTURING CORP.

Area	Population	% Participation	Customer Count	Check Average	Estimated Sales	
					Daily	Annual
Plant Cafeteria						
Shift No. 1						
Shift No. 2						
Shift No. 3						
Office Cafeteria						
Shift No. 1						
Shift No. 2						
Shift No. 3						
Dining Rooms						
Foreman						
Executive						
TOTAL						

Whether the office works five days or six days, and whether the dining rooms are operated other than at lunch or on weekends, must be taken into consideration when projecting total sales.

The Budget Presentation

The remainder of the budget presentation for the Rural Manufacturing Co. would follow the same pattern prescribed for the Urban Office Building Corp. in Case History No. 1. Backup information in the form of breakdowns and schedule for payroll man/hours costs, food cost and other direct operating expenses are identical in style.

The summary should follow the accounting statement format of the plant. If the facility is company operated, this would be as a department of the plant. If the unit is caterer operated, this would be as a separate accounting statement of a unit.

Other Income

It is common for the vending share of sales in a manufacturing plant to pay a percentage of sales as a commission to the plant. Chapter X on foodservice vending describes this in greater detail. When vending machines are used to provide the "break" service to a plant, they decrease cafeteria sales of hot and cold beverages, the most profitable portion of the cafeteria sales mix. In such a case, the foodservice manager should make every effort as a matter of policy to assure that vending commissions are credited to the cafeteria statement as *other income* to overcome cafeteria costs.

Internal politics in the average plant often give the vending commissions to union welfare or slush funds, employee funds and various other funds. A successful manager of a plant foodservice must keep management constantly aware that vending sales are foodservice sales and should be combined in the profit or loss column with the employee cafeteria.

CASE HISTORY NUMBER 3—COMMUNITY HOSPITAL

As the industrial foodservice manager takes on the position of "hospital" foodservice manager, his approach to buying, preparing and serving food must change in a marked degree from that required for a manufacturing plant or office building complex. While he has the same management problems of ordering, receiving, preparing and "dishing up" meals and the related problems of hiring, supervising and directing the efforts of the work force who handle the food preparation, he now must add to his responsibility for the employee cafeteria and the executive dining area a third service—"the patient meal." In addition, he may also operate a retail foodservice, the coffee shop.

Budgeting for these operations assumes a new dimension and will require a completely different set of terms on the accounting statement. The base terminology used in a hospital foodservice is *cost per patient day*. All the costs of a hospital are based on this cost per patient day structure.

In recent years, the federal government has instituted the Medicare and Medicaid programs. These forms of government reimbursement to hospitals for services performed necessitate complicated accounting procedures for the hospital field. They are quite similar to the cost accounting systems used in the hotel industry.

Each department of a hospital has its own departmental budget. The foodservice (dietary department) must budget for three main areas of cost:

1. Food
2. Labor
3. Supplies

There is seldom any other breakdown of cost similar to those used in the normal accounting codes of the Business and Industry type of accounting statement. In most instances, sales income from food sold in the employee cafeteria is credited against the purchase of all food and the labor required to operate the cafeteria remains as part of the dietary labor cost.

Page 18 of Chapter III shows a typical format for a hospital budget. The index of a hospital budget as prepared by a foodservice manager should be similar to the following breakdown:

I.   Introduction—Statement of Policy
II.   Projection of Patient Days
III.   Projection of Cafeteria Income
IV.   Projection of Food Cost
V.   Labor Cost—Man/Hours Projection
VI.   Supplies Cost Projection
VII.   Summary
VIII. Recommendations

As the budget is prepared, the same opportunity to state policy and make recommendations exists in preparing parts I and VIII as is found in the preparation of budgets discussed previously. However, the text of the budget discussion takes on a different tone; the following is an example of how a hospital budget would be worded and compiled.

1. Introduction—Statement of Policy

This portion of the budget should state the services that must be performed; the expected low, high and average number of patient days that are anticipated and should generally set the stage for the hospital administrator to evaluate the dietary budget. It should read something like this:

> The following budget material has been prepared based on an expected patient day occupancy of Community Hospital of 350-450 patients with an annual average of 410 patients.
>
> The present two-week cycle menu will be continued.
>
> The present employee cafeteria will operate for four meals a day (breakfast, lunch, dinner and midnight meal) and will be closed at all other hours.
>
> The kitchen will provide prepared food for the coffee shop but the women's auxiliary will operate that facility. An inter-department transfer will reimburse the kitchen for the cost of the food provided.

This clearly states the "service" portion of the objective on which the "financial" portion will be based.

II. Projection of Patient Days

Since the main effort performed by the dietary department will be to feed the hospital patient, a projection of the number of patients to be fed must be made. Hospital administrative offices keep excellent records of these figures and they are easily obtainable. A survey of information available should be made and presented. Comparative studies on a month by month basis, projection of trends, and other similar methods are all acceptable. Assistance can be obtained from the Administrator's office.

The total hospital budget is being planned on a "patient day" basis and the foodservice manager should have little difficulty in coordinating his plans to that figure, but it should be restated at this point of the budget.

III. Projection of Cafeteria Income

Many employee cafeterias in hospitals sell food to the hospital employees at or near a 100% food cost. Some try to recover part of the extra labor cost involved, but that is the exception rather than the rule. A survey of the previous year's cafeteria sales figure can serve to project the next year's income and that figure should be included in this section for comparison purposes. The format used in Case Histories No. 1 and No. 2 can also be used for operations whose price structures are above food cost and where customer count and check averages by meal period are the criteria for estimating sales.

IV. Projection of Food Cost

Projection of food cost in a hospital differs from the method used for a retail sales location. The hospital patient is a "boarding" guest who eats three meals a day and is usually provided juice or other beverages twice a day in addition to his three meals. Hospital menus are standardized (see Chapter XI on menus) and can be costed out easily. In order to establish the budgeted food cost of a dietary department, the following should be accomplished:

1. Cost out the cycle menus that are being used and estimate the average cost per patient day.

2. Evaluate the average cost of employee meals per day and divide this figure by the average annual patient days.

3. Add the two costs
    a) Patient meals daily cost
    b) Employee meals cost divided by patient days

The sum of these two figures provides the average food cost per patient day for both patient and employee meals.

4. Multiply the figure from 3 above by the annual estimated patient days and arrive at annual cost per patient for food.

V. Labor Cost and Man/Hours Projection

A schedule of labor should be prepared identical to that shown in Case History Number 1. In addition, annual wages should be evaluated. This is done by adding the number of weeks of vacation to the annual 52 weeks to determine annual wages because, in most cases, replacements must be hired to fill vacation schedules for a hospital, since it operates seven days a week all year. Different areas have different vacation policies. Many unionized hospitals have up to four weeks vacation per year and this must be considered when projecting payroll costs.

Payroll related costs should be projected the same as for Case History Number 1 and added to total labor costs.

VI. Supplies Cost Projection

Supplies cost in a hospital usually covers paper goods and cleaning supplies. Usually most of the other materials are included in the janitorial or the other cost centers of the hospital budget. Some hospitals use an abundance of disposable service and some still use very few disposables. A survey should be made of the actual cost of paper goods and cleaning supplies for at least one month and then projected on a one-year basis.

VII. Summary

All the foregoing information should be summarized in the accounting language of the hospital. This should result in a statement that looks something like the illustration on the next page, Fig. 10.

VIII. Recommendations

This section of the budget format should follow the same presentation as in Case History Number 1. The foodservice manager should insert all of his ideas and recommendations for improving service and/or cutting costs at this point. Often an improvement in overall service, although it costs money and increases the cost per patient day, will be approved if the administration feels it will benefit the hospital.

Much of a hospital's costs are paid for by Blue Cross, Medicare, Medicaid and other forms of insurance. An efficient hospital food manager becomes familiar with these insurance plans and provides the best possible service at a cost within reason. Once costs are budgeted and approved, the money is available to spend, but a low budget that results in poor food or poor service leads to feelings of dissatisfaction that will continue to haunt the manager for the entire year.

CASE HISTORY NUMBER 4–CAMPUS UNIVERSITY

Budgeting for the college foodservice combines some of the elements of budgeting for the plant or office building with elements of hospital foodservice budgeting. Chapter III, example 3, cites a campus type college with a student cafeteria serving contract meals to boarding students and cash meals to transient students, as well as a faculty dining room and a snack bar. This could conceivably require three separate monthly accounting statements summarized on a fourth statement showing the combined status of the financial condition of the total foodservice each month. The standard definition for budget format applies here:

The budget format should follow the exact pattern of the monthly accounting statement.

Fig. 10–COMMUNITY HOSPITAL
DIETARY DEPT. BUDGET

Estimated Annual Patient Days

        @ 410 per day average   149,650

Gross Food Purchases	$289,621	
Less Cafeteria Sales	$ 74,125	
Net Food Cost	$215,496	
Food Cost per patient day		$1.44

Total Payroll and Payroll		
Related Costs	$344,195	
Labor Cost per patient day		$2.30

Supplies Cost	$ 41,902	
Supplies Cost per patient day		$ .28

Total Dietary Dept. Cost	$601,593	

Dietary Dept. Cost per patient day		$4.02

(These figures are based on an actual location in New York City in 1970.)

For the purpose of this case history and to provide a method of presenting the budget for a specific set of circumstances, the following criteria are established:

1. The student cafeteria will show as income the sale of all student meal contracts and the cash sales to all transient students.

2. The faculty dining room will show sales to regular cafeteria income and costs to regular cafeteria costs.

3. The snack bar will be operated as a separate enterprise, supported by the cafeteria kitchens acting as a "commissary" but keeping separate books and records. Profits will be used to offset student activities and will not accrue to the cafeteria.

4. Commissions from vending operations will accrue to the student cafeteria as "other income" to offset operating costs.

The index of such a budget should look like this:

Note that the method of presentation combines information and style of presentation similar to that contained in Case Histories No. 1, No. 2 and No. 3. Let's review them point by point:

I. Introduction

Here, again, a statement of policy, as you understand it or desire it to be, is presented. This statement should include:

a) Policy on the number of weekly meals provided to a boarding student. Some schools offer 5-day, 6-day or 7-day contracts at 15, 18 or 21 meals. This must be clarified and understood.

b) Policy of pricing "a la carte" sales to non-boarding students. The basic philosophy should be to make the price structure such that all students will prefer to purchase meal contracts.

c) Policy on hours of operation. The number of hours the cafeteria is kept in operation should be as limited as possible.

d) Policy on "free seconds." The trend in today's colleges is to allow the contract student "all he can eat," with some minor exceptions among menu items, (i.e. steak, roast beef, etc.) This is an extremely important point.

e) Pricing policy for special affairs. Many colleges use the student foodservice as a central point for catering. This is a good source of income when the pricing policy is right but a drain on costs when the pricing policy is wrong.

f. Other relevant and similar material.

As with the first three case histories, the budget introduction should cover as much basic information as possible to establish the ground rules of policy.

II. Sales Projection

In this case history, income (sales) is derived from:
1. Student contracts
2. Student retail sales
3. Faculty dining
4. Sales of food to snack bar
5. Catering

Income as commissions from vending machines is not sales, but will show up later as "other income."

An analysis of each category of potential sales income is made using a format similar to Case Histories No. 1 and No. 2 plus additions to suit the college situations. Here is how such a format would look:

Category	No. of Potential Customers	% Partic.	Aver. Weekly Customers	Est. Check Average	Est. Sales Weekly	Est. Annual Sales
Student Contracts	_____	_____	_____	_____	_____	$_____
Transient Students	_____	_____	_____	_____	_____	$_____
Faculty	_____	_____	_____	_____	_____	$_____
Catering	_____	_____	_____	_____	_____	$_____
Food Transfers	_____	_____	_____	_____	_____	$_____
				Total Estimated Annual Sales		$_____

Special attention must be paid to the number of "sales" days in the year. The average school year has 150 days (2 15-week semesters) for students, with some summer activity. Faculty are usually present for an additional period and the snack bar operates on a different basis. Each category must be analyzed separately.

III. Food Cost Projection

Food costs will vary for each category of sales and must be evaluated separately. For student contracts, evaluation should cover the average actual food cost of a meal, less the expected average absenteeism factors.

Transient student sales will reflect the usual food cost ratio to sales picture, as is normal with any retail sales transaction.

Faculty dining rooms often have menus priced at a more attractive level than the student cafeteria and food cost for this portion of projected sales must be calculated at that level.

Food transfers to the snack bar are usually very close to cost and must be projected accordingly.

As a result, a table of food cost expectations by sales category must be made in a manner similar to the following:

Category	Proj. Annual Sales	Proj. % Food Cost	Proj. Food Cost Dollars
Contract Student	$_____	_____ %	$_____
Transient Student	$_____	_____ %	$_____
Faculty	$_____	_____ %	$_____
Catering	$_____	_____ %	$_____
Food Transfers	$_____	_____ %	$_____
Total	$_____	_____ %	$_____

The resulting total will provide the overall food cost to sales ratio of the "sales" portion of the budget.

IV. Labor Cost Projection

A complete survey identical to that shown for Case History No. 1 should be presented. While Case History No. 1 shows all employees at 52 weeks per year, a school/college survey should evaluate the number of weeks that all personnel work. While the manager and key personnel will be employed 52 weeks per year, a major portion of the rank and file will be employed as hourly paid workers and only work when school is in session.

The format for assembling annual labor costs for a school/college situation appears on the next page, Fig. 11.

V. Payroll Related Costs

The same method used in Case History No. 1 should be used to project payroll related costs. Special consideration should be given to the unemployment insurance rate which may be higher than normal due to seasonal layoffs every year, causing a higher unemployment insurance rate. (See Chapter XV on insurance). Additional attention must be given to the number of paid holidays and other special payroll-related benefit programs that can exist in a school/college situation.

VI. Direct Operating Expenses

The rule "Follow the format of the accounting statement" must be given close attention in the school/college situation. It is not unusual to find allocations being charged against the

Fig. 11–SUMMARY OF ANNUAL LABOR COSTS

Job Title	No. of Employees	Weekly Man/Hours	Wage Rate	Total Weekly Est.	No. of Weeks Per Yr.	Total Annual Est.
I. Administrative						
Manager	1	48	250	250	52	
Asst. Manager	1	48	175	175	52	
Clerk	1	40	125	125	52	
Subtotal						

II. Production Personnel

Chefs
Cooks
Kitchen Men
Bakers
Dishwashers

Unless there is summer school and some part of the facility open all year, these would be 30 week-per-year personnel.

III. Faculty Dining Room

Waitresses
Utility/Bus

Same comments as for II–Production Personnel.

IV. Sanitation

Head Utility
Utility

It is likely that some maintenance and clean up would be performed in "off school" periods. Personnel must be evaluated accordingly.

SUMMARY

I

II

III

IV

Estimated Total Weekly Payroll During School Sessions $

Estimated Annual Payroll $

_____% Reserve for wage increases $

Total Budgeted Payroll $

foodservice for utilities, rent, garbage removal, air-conditioning and other such items. While the paper goods, cleaning supplies, laundry and replacement figures are controllable by the foodservice manager and, therefore, are predictable for budgeting, the other direct charges, which may be applied by the administration or the accounting department, must be sought out and included in the budget. An effective manager checks, double checks and then qualifies his statement as shown in the introduction portion of the budget.

VIII. Summary

The summary portion of the budget should recapitulate all the supporting information into a projected annual statement. At this point, vending commissions are shown as other income after all sales and costs are listed. The following is a typical summary statement.

Fig. 12—COLLEGE SUMMARY STATEMENT

I. *Sales*

Student contracts		$_____
Cash cafeteria sales (inc. faculty)		$_____
Other sales		$_____
	Total sales income	$_____

II. *Costs*

Food Cost		$_____
Payroll and related costs		$_____
	Total food and payroll	$_____

III. *Direct Expenses*

Paper goods		$_____
Cleaning supplies		$_____
Laundry		$_____
(List all others)		
	Total direct expenses	$_____
	Total all costs	$_____
Other income (vending commissions)		$_____
	Net profit (or loss)	$_____

Should the projected statement show a profit, the administration may decide to maintain the current rate for students and eliminate the profit. Should the projected statement show a loss, the administration may decide to increase the boarding rate and/or the cash sale selling prices.

Under either circumstance, a unit manager, having presented a complete and precise budget, is in a position to guide policy and decisions to the point where he can establish a clear definition of the financial obligation for the coming school year.

FACT GATHERING SYSTEMS FOR BUDGETING

All of the budget case histories follow the same theme:

1. *A budget must be prepared.*
2. *The budget should follow the accounting format of the organization.*

All too often the thought of having to gather the necessary facts to prepare a budget—plus the task of writing it up to provide a completed document—intimidates the unit operating manager. If sufficient information is not in existence to be intelligently analyzed, a comprehensive budget cannot be prepared. The most useful fact gathering tool for assembling all the necessary fiscal information required for budget preparation is the weekly operating report. Chapter IX discusses the report in depth. A manager's intelligent overview of this report, linking its immediate use as a cost control tool to its long range use as a budget preparation tool, is a key ingredient to successful budget preparation.

VI: The Personnel Cycle

In industry, the management of people is often described as the "Personnel Function." Some management consultants have stated that "Personnel management *is* management." There are enough books written on the subject of personnel management to fill a goodly number of library shelves; material on specialized topics and sub-specialized topics is available in abundance. Clearly, it would be impossible to provide in one chapter of a book such as this a comprehensive course in personnel management; instead this chapter will attempt to orient the industrial foodservice manager to the basic "cycle of personnel."

THE PERSONNEL CYCLE

All facets of business have a definite "cycle" of events and the personnel function is no exception. Each step in the personnel cycle involves definite management practices that when properly executed can assist the industrial foodservice manager in achieving his overall objectives. This "cycle" can be defined as follows:
1) Recruiting
2) Interviewing
3) Hiring
4) Training
5) Supervising
6) Evaluating
7) Termination

Recruiting

Today's foodservice personnel come from all walks of life with differing educational backgrounds. Many foodservice positions require little formal education (such as dish washer) while others require special skills and training (cashier, short order cook, etc.) Recruiting means locating the right person for the position available. The ability to locate someone who has the skills, talent, education and temperament to fill your vacancy is the first step towards good personnel management.

In order to intelligently recruit for a position, you must first know what you are expecting from the person who will fill the job. Determining job expectations is accomplished by preparing a job description. There are numerous books on this subject and a good industrial foodservice manager owns and continually explores at least one such book. A job description is shown below but a detailed description of its preparation is not included. The steps required in the preparation of job descriptions are left for other courses of study. Suffice it to say that every industrial foodservice operations unit should have a job description written for every job/position on its staff as a pre-requisite for recruiting. This can be accomplished independently or with the assistance of the next level of supervision above you, or job descriptions can be provided for you by that same supervisor.

JOB DESCRIPTION

POSITION TITLE:	Grill Attendant/Cook's Helper
JOB NUMBER:	GR-4
DEPARTMENT:	Production
REPORTS TO:	Chef
RESPONSIBILITIES:	Responsible for quality of food independently prepared.
	Responsible for sanitation in area of work.
DUTIES:	Prepare menu items assigned.
	Assist Chef in preparation of soups, sauces, gravies, meats, poultry and fish.
	Assist when assigned in vegetable section in peeling, paring and cutting of vegetables.
	Assist in cleaning kitchen equipment and tools.
EDUCATION:	Apprenticeship in culinary arts training.
EXPERIENCE:	Three years in foodservice production work.

If you are employed by one of the major industrial catering companies, your district manager is the next level of supervision and should be able to assist you in preparing job descriptions or to provide them for you as part of his responsibility.

If you are employed directly by an industrial company, school or hospital, this is a personnel function and there will be a department head who can assist you in meeting this need. No matter what course you take in their preparation, you should have job descriptions available as the primary tool in recruiting applicants.

The unit manager must be thoroughly familiar with the job description and have a full understanding of the job he is recruiting for if he is to be effective in locating and hiring the correct person for each vacancy that may exist.

Sources for recruiting vary from place to place as well as from company to caterer.
EXAMPLE
If you are employed as foodservice manager in a plant or factory in a company-operated

foodservice, you would use the plant personnel department to recruit workers—
BUT

If you were employed in the same position for a catering company, you would use that company's personnel department to recruit workers—
BUT

If neither source proved successful, you might place a "want ad" in a local paper or contact a personnel agency in the area that specializes in culinary personnel in order to recruit workers.

In all three instances, the recruiting source will merely provide you with "potential" employees, and the selection process is up to you as manager. Your ability to select the proper person brings you to the second step in the personnel cycle.

Interviewing

After you have decided what position you want filled and what the person employed in that position must do, you are faced with the task of interviewing applicants and deciding which ones you will hire and which ones you will reject as unsuitable. Here are some helpful hints to good interviewing:

1. Immediately prior to interviewing, re-read the job description and have it in front of you at the time of the interview. The primary question you should be asking yourself during the interview is: *"Can* and *will* this applicant, if hired, fulfill the needs listed in the job description?" If the answer to that question turns out to be "No," terminate the interview quickly in a respectful manner. If the answer to that question turns out to be "Yes," continue to evaluate the applicant and rate him against other applicants for the same position, selecting the most desirable candidate for the job.

2. Prior to spending time on the interview, have the applicant fill out a standard application form. Whether you work for a caterer or a company, hospital or school, they all have application forms. By reviewing the data the prospective employee writes on the application form, you have an additional source of information to compare with the needs of the job description.

3. Conduct each interview in a polite, businesslike manner. Make an effort to put the applicant at his ease so he will react normally to your questioning. A nervous applicant will give a poor impression and most applicants are nervous at the start of an interview. Your ability to establish a comfortable atmosphere will allow you to learn what you want to know about your applicant.

4. Using the job description, compare the personality traits, skills, and/or his past experience with the needs of the job. Be sure to ask yourself the "Yes-No" questions described in 1 above and try to come up with an honest answer.

5. If you intend to hire the applicant, fully discuss the job conditions and make sure that they are acceptable to him. These should include:

a) Wages
b) Work Schedule (hours)
c) Days Off
d) Meals and Uniforms
e) Possibility for Advancement/Promotion
f) Means of travel to and from work
g) Employee benefits
h) Union affiliation (if any)
i) Other similar information

Remember that the more the applicant knows about the job and the company he will work for, the less he will be surprised after you hire him.

6. Provide sufficient uninterrupted time for the interview. This will allow you to learn as much as possible about the applicant and assist you in selection. Interruptions or short answers do both yourself and the applicant a disservice.

7. Treat the applicant with the same respect and courtesy you would expect if you were applying for a job. Remember that the interview is the first meeting between two people and the applicant is getting his first impression of you just as you are getting your first impression of him. Should you ultimately hire him, you want his initial impression to be favorable. Should you not hire him, you want him to leave feeling he was fairly evaluated but just did not get the job. You do not want him to speak poorly of either you or your company in the community where you will be seeking other applicants in the future.

Some of the "dont's" for interviewing—common pitfalls that many a manager falls into—should be guarded against. These are:

Don't do two things at once. Interviewing requires all your attention. Don't take deliveries, talk on the telephone, serve customers, make sandwiches, check out the cash register or do other routine tasks while you are interviewing. If you haven't the time now, give the applicant an application to fill out and ask him to wait or return at a time when you can properly interview.

Don't be disrespectful or impolite. Remember that your own personal reputation is on the line every time you conduct an interview.

Don't misrepresent. If undesirable tasks are required, either occasionally or daily, tell the employee during the interview that they are part of the job. Remember that in every foodservice someone has to wash the pots and handle the garbage and it is better to have the prospective employee know what he must do *before* he starts work than to have him quit the first week after he finds out.

Don't underestimate him. Don't underestimate the trouble a new employee can cause if he is militant or disrespectful to others or has personal qualities not compatible to your needs. While color and race are not important, manners and attitude are. Pay particular attention to his personality and personal habits.

There are many more items that could be listed, but at this point by giving the matter some thought, in line with the principles of management, you should be able to provide your own checklist for interviewing and it will be designed to suit your own taste and needs. With the proper forethought and planning and review of the above, your interviewing efforts should result in selecting the best people available for the job openings in your unit.

Hiring

After you have completed the interview and selected the new employee, he is then "hired" and you initiate the administrative process that places him on the payroll. At this point you have both governmental obligations and internal company policy obligations to fulfill. State and Federal laws require that the new employee fill out the necessary income tax information forms; U. S. Dept. of Labor and trade union regulations require that he be provided such things as time cards, locker, etc.; and your own company's rules usually require forms to place the new employee's name on the payroll data processing record. You should also have a personnel "jacket" file on each employee and this must be initiated. A short check list should be made and used to assure that all has been accomplished, and should include, but not be limited to, the following:

1. Complete and fill out income tax forms (W-2 for the Federal government and possibly some state or local forms also).

2. Insurance or employee benefit forms, as may be applicable.

3. Trade union applications, or information, where they are required.

4. Initial payroll information form to place employee's name in the data processing or manual system.

5. Employee time card, or enter name in a time book.

6. Initiate personnel file or jacket, as may be standard practice in your unit.

7. Provide locker key and uniform issued with signature for responsibility.

Other items can be added to this list to suit your need, but these seven are a minimum.

Placing Employees on Job

"Hiring" has other facets than just these administrative steps. These additional actions can be termed "placing the employee on the job." Be sure to:

1. Show the employee how to get into the plant, office building, etc. There are often security measures and passes he must use.

2. Show him where he checks in, whether by time clock or time book. Some manufacturing plants have elaborate data processing systems, while some industrial locations have a simple register called a time book.

3. Introduce him to his supervisor and other employees he will work with.

4. Take him to his job location and assign a specific employee or supervisor to show him the specific tasks of his share of the unit work load.

5. Follow up at the end of the first day to make sure that he has "heard" and "absorbed" what was said and shown to him.

Remember your own first day on the new job and you will know what your new employee is thinking. *The first day is the critical day.* Many a new employee turns out to be good or poor depending on that "first day."

If there is an employee handbook for your location, an information or insurance booklet, or other written data about his job or benefits, hand it to him on the way out the first day. You'd be amazed at the difference in results based on the timing in handing out this material. On the way IN, it often is left on a locker shelf in the excitement of the new job; on the way OUT, it is usually read on the way home or at home after he has had a day's experience to relate to it.

Training

Training is changed behavior. If behavior doesn't change, training has not taken place.

After the hiring of a new employee has been completed, some form of training must take place to teach him the job skills he will need for his job or to make his previously acquired skills compatible to his new job.

The period of training will vary with the complexity of the job and the ability of the employee. The results of training will vary with the amount of sincere effort you as a unit manager will expend and the value you place on the training function.

Here, again, the subject is too complex to cover in a single chapter of a "general" book on foodservice management. Outside study and personal improvement on a continuing basis are required to become truly effective at employee training. At this point it is enough to make you aware that training is a definite step in the personnel cycle and that you must do something about becoming proficient at accomplishing it.

Supervising

After you have completed hiring and training your new employee, the task of day-to-day supervision of his efforts follows. A manager is usually involved in all phases of the personnel cycle at the same time; training new employees while supervising old employees on the same shift is normal.

Supervising means directing the efforts of your employees to accomplish their assigned tasks. Since customer count, menu variety, and service needs change from time to time, assigned tasks also change accordingly. While an employee's basic assignment may stay constant, portions of production, set-up and clean-up as well as work loads change daily in most operations.

EXAMPLE
  1. A menu with roast meat requires little preparation or production effort.
  2. A menu with beef stew requires extensive pre-preparation effort.
  3. A menu with beef pot pie requires still more pre-preparation effort plus production changes.
Other areas of operations experience similar changes in their daily routines and supervision is required to assure that your staff adjusts their efforts to meet these daily needs.

Don't assume that your employees will perform effectively if left alone. All foodservice employees require continuing interest and supervision on the part of the manager to perform at maximum effectiveness.

Remember, supervising means directing the efforts of others. Here are some aids to being a good supervisor:

Make orders sound like requests, but mean business. By your tone and manner, make your employees *want* to accomplish assigned tasks, no matter how distasteful the task is. Don't forget that someone must wash pots and handle garbage in our industry.

Be sure all directions are concise and clear. If your employees do not fully understand what you want done, they cannot effectively accomplish it.

Say "Thank You." Each human being wants to enjoy the feeling of accomplishment; as your employees accomplish *your* goals, find some way to show *your* pleasure. There are many ways to say "Thank you" without using the specific words. Learn them and use them.

Don't request the impossible. Some employees are less capable than others. Don't request an employee to accomplish a task that he is not capable of. Assign that task to a worker who can accomplish it. A good example is money handling. When assigned as cashier, many a good cafeteria worker "freezes" at the thought of handling and being responsible for money. Know your employees. Learn their limitations and capabilities.

Remember the Golden Rule. "Do unto others as you would have them do unto you." *It's still a good rule* and the best way to get things done.

Evaluating

Every employee wants to know how he stands with his boss and an employee is entitled to this information on a periodic basis. This is especially important for a new employee after the early days of his new job.

In some situations, where the foodservice employees are members of a trade union, employers are given 30 or 60 days to evaluate a new employee before he joins the union and during that period can dismiss him without fear of a union reprisal. Once the new employee is "accepted" by his employer and joins the union, the employer must then abide by all the terms of the union contract, including wage increases and dismissals. Evaluation becomes an important step in the personnel cycle where this situation exists. Evaluation of an employee's performance need not be complicated; however, based on the level of the employee's position, evaluation takes on different meanings.

EXAMPLE:

1. Evaluating a dishwasher's performance merely means evaluating reliability and effort.

2. Evaluating a cook's performance requires consideration of skill and technical knowledge as well.

3. Evaluating a supervisor's performance also takes into consideration the ability to direct cooks and dishwashers and to obtain the proper result from their efforts.

There are many forms described in personnel management books that can be adopted or modified for your use in evaluating employees; two forms are especially important: one for "rank and file" personnel and one for "supervisory" personnel. Two forms that I use for this purpose appear on pp. 56 and 58, Fig. 13, p. 56 can be used for hourly employees and Fig. 14, pp. 57, 58 can be used for supervisors.

If an operation has a trade union shop, an evaluation form on the new employee should surely be prepared before he enters the union (this is usually 30 days after the date he was hired). If the employee evaluates as "unsatisfactory," immediate action should be taken to assure that he does not become a "permanent" union employee.

In the case of non-union locations, a program of evaluation and appraisal should be made a part of the personnel policy of the operation.

If you are employed as a manager for a major catering company, such a policy will surely exist and be available to you. Your district manager will be responsible for seeing that you enforce the policy that exists and should assist you in becoming proficient at preparing evaluations of your employees. In most instances, a request for a wage increase by you for an employee must be accompanied by an evaluation or appraisal presented either informally or on a specific form.

If you are employed as a manager directly by a company, school or hospital, they usually have a policy covering employee evaluations with which you should be familiar.

As you complete the "hiring" process for a new employee, you should mark your calendar thirty days later for a "Review of John Smith" and then evaluate his performance at that time. You should again ask yourself the question "*Can* and *will* this employee continually perform his job?" If for any reason the answer comes up "No," you have the distasteful task of terminating him. Any employee found not satisfactory at the 30-day point should be earmarked for training as a potentially satisfactory employee or should be terminated as soon as possible. To procrastinate or continue to retain an employee who cannot or will not carry his fair share of the work load is to invite trouble with the rest of your staff. Evaluation is the tool for making the go-no go decision.

Termination–Resignation

Periodically, it becomes necessary to terminate an undesirable employee or to accept the resignation or transfer of a desirable employee. Under either circumstance you have become involved with administrative procedures to de-activate all the functions you activated when he was hired. Payroll forms, insurance forms, time cards and similar items all come into play again at this time. If you have kept an efficient current employee file, you will have little difficulty. However, if you have been negligent in maintaining your employee records, you will have trouble.

The "check list" system described in relation to other areas discussed in this chapter is quite applicable to an employee separation. You should have such a check list and use it when separating an employee from your unit, regardless of the reason he is leaving. Here is a sample of some items that should be on your list.

1. Are all items that were issued returned?
    a) Locker key
    b) Knives, other hand tools
    c) Uniforms
    d) Passes, badges, etc.
2. Have security measures been completed? (This is especially applicable if your food operation services a government plant or factory.)
3. Inspect employee locker for sanitation and company property.
4. Complete all forms for unemployment insurance possibilities.
5. Complete personnel forms that may be used by your employer to discontinue employee benefits.
6. Advise departing employee of possible insurance continuation or termination.
7. Complete the employee's personnel jacket or file and place in "Old Employees" section of your files.

Many other items can be added to this list. You should be aware that many requests will arrive at your unit for information about previous employees and only well kept records of employment and conditions of termination can provide the answers. You may be required to provide to local or national governmental agencies at a later date, information that is required by law; or union information as part of a labor agreement; insurance information to keep from paying an expensive claim or other similar data. By observing good administrative practices in putting your records "to bed" on a separated employee, you are following good personnel management practices.

Review

Personnel management *is* management. Learning and following proper procedures as briefly outlined in this review of the personnel cycle are among the most important tasks a manager performs.

If you become adept at personnel management, and learn the personnel policies and procedures of your company or industrial employer, you will be well on your way to being a good manager in the areas of man/hours planning and manpower utilization.

If you *recruit, interview, hire, train, supervise* and *evaluate* well, all your *terminations* will be resignations or transfers and you will be spared the unpleasant task of dismissing employees. If you continually improve your personnel management abilities through self-study and practice, you will develop the base for future promotion and success. Your employees are your greatest resource as a manager and the only resource that offers unlimited potential. Your ability to motivate their efforts using good personnel management techniques can be the secret ingredient to success as an industrial foodservice manager.

Fig. 13–HOURLY EMPLOYEE APPRAISAL FORM

<u>HOURLY EMPLOYEE APPRAISAL FORM</u>

UNIT NAME   UNIT NO.   DATE

EMPLOYEE NAME _____   CLOCK NUMBER _____

PRESENT WAGES: _____ PRESENT POSITION: _____

STARTING DATE: _____ 30 DAYS UP ON: _____ MGR. SIGNATURE _____

1. QUALITY OF WORK Does Quality Meet Recognized Standard?	GOOD		AVERAGE		POOR	
	Remarks:					

2. PRODUCTIVITY Amount Of "Output" of Employee.	HIGH		AVERAGE		LOW	
	Remarks:					

3. APPLICATION TO JOB How Well Does Employee Apply Himself To The Task At Hand?	GOOD		AVERAGE		POOR	
	Remarks:					

4. RATE OF LEARNING	GOOD		AVERAGE		POOR	
	Remarks:					

5. VERSATILITY Can Employee Fill Several Positions Satisfactory?	HIGH		AVERAGE		LOW	
	Remarks:					

6. SUPERVISION Amount Of Supervision Required.	LESS THAN AVERAGE		AVERAGE		MORE THAN AVERAGE	
	Remarks:					

7. TEAM WORK Does Employee Work Well With A Group?	GOOD		AVERAGE		POOR	
	Remarks:					

8. ATTITUDE What Is Employee's General Attitude?	VERY COOPERATIVE		SATISFACTORY		UN-COOPER-ATIVE	
	Remarks:					

OVERALL JOB PERFORMANCE

BELOW AVERAGE [ ]   AVERAGE [ ]   VERY SATISFACTORY [ ]

Recommendations & Remarks: _____

_____

_____

_____

_____

APPROVED FOR UNION ACCEPTANCE

_____
MANAGER'S SIGNATURE

Fig. 14—SUPERVISORS APPRAISAL REPORT

Name _____   Position _____   Time in Position _____

Present Wage _____   Service Date _____

SECTION I

Consider employee's performance in PRESENT POSITION. Place check mark in MIDDLE OF MOST APPLICABLE BLOCK, or ON **APPROPRIATE LINE BETWEEN BLOCKS** if appraisal on any item is intermediate. If wording is not adequate, or if additional comment is necessary, amplify in "Remarks" section.

1. KNOWLEDGE OF WORK: Understanding of all phases of his work and related matters.	Needs instruction or guidance.	Has required knowledge	Has thorough knowledge of own and related work.
	Remarks:		
2. VOLUME OF WORK: Quantity of acceptable work.	Should be increased	Regularly meets recognized standards.	Unusually high output.
	Remarks:		
3. QUALITY OF WORK: Thoroughness, neatness, and accuracy of work.	Needs improvement.	Regularly meets recognized standards.	Consistently maintains highest quality.
	Remarks:		
4. PERSONALITY: Effect on other people as a result of his disposition, tact, enthusiasm, sincerity, appearance, etc.	Sometimes creates unfavorable impression.	Well liked and accepted.	Outstanding. A splendid influence.
	Remarks:		
5. ANALYTICAL ABILITY: Ability to size up a problem, get and evaluate the facts, reach sound conclusions and present them in clear and concise manner.	Has difficulty.	Meets required standards.	Especially able.
	Remarks:		
6. JUDGMENT The degree to which decisions or actions are sound.	Occasionally faulty.	Reliable.	Excellent.
	Remarks:		
7. MENTAL ALERTNESS: Ability to interpret and respond to instructions, new situations, methods and procedures.	Slow to comprehend.	Readily understands.	Exceptionally wide awake and alert
	Remarks:		
8. INITIATIVE: Ability to originate or develop constructive ideas and to take necessary steps to get things done.	Follows precedent.	Has necessary drive.	Unusually resourceful.
	Remarks:		
9. COOPERATION: Ability and willingness to work with and for others toward best interests of all concerned.	Inclined to be inconsiderate of others.	Good teamworker.	Exceptionally cooperative.
	Remarks:		
10. PLANNING AND ORGANIZING: Ability to plan ahead, schedule and lay out work so as to make most effective use of personnel, materials and equipment.	Needs assistance.	Plans and organizes well.	Very effective under all conditions.
	Remarks:		
11. LEADERSHIP: Ability to inspire in others the willingness and desire toward a given objective.	Has difficulty.	Gets results without friction.	Inspiring and effective leader.
	Remarks:		
12. DEVELOPMENT OF SUBORDINATES Recognition and development of the aptitudes, abilities, and capacities of others.	Contributes but little to their development.	Successful in recognizing and developing the possibilities of others.	Very capable and active in developing his men.
	Remarks:		*(cont.)*

Fig. 14–SUPERVISORS APPRAISAL REPORT (cont.)

SECTION II

1. Concerning his present assignment
   a. Is this man properly placed?_____
      If not, explain briefly_____
      _____

   b. Does he need further training and development to improve performance?_____
      If so, what?_____
      _____

   c. Indicate by circle his overall job performance:

      Below Average   Average   Above Average–Very Satisfactory

   d. Recommendations and remarks: _____
      _____
      _____
      _____

      Prepared by_____ In consultation with_____

SECTION III

1. Reviewed with employee on_____ By_____
   Comments:_____
   _____
   _____

2. Concerning his future:
   a. What are his outstanding abilities (assignments on which he has excelled, etc.)?_____
      _____

   b. What are his weak points (Personal characteristics or assignments on which he has not proved
      satisfactory, etc.)? _____
      _____

   c. For what types of work has he a decided personal leaning or preference?_____
      _____

   d. Is he interested Food Service as a Career?_____
      What type of work?_____
   e. For what type assignment does he appear a candidate for advancement in present or other
      department or subsidiary: _____
         1. Next Assignment?_____
         2. Eventual? _____
   f. When will he be ready for next assignment indicated? _____
   g. What training or experience is necessary meanwhile to qualify him for such next assignment?
      _____
      _____

   h. Remarks: _____
      _____

_____   _____   _____   _____
                                                      Manager   Division Executive

VII: Man/Hours Planning for Industrial Foodservice

The building blocks of knowledge needed for the task of man/hours planning have been provided in the preceding chapters as briefly noted here—

Chapter III described the operating goal as:

      1. Financial Limitations (Money)
      2. Service Requirements (Need)

Chapter IV discussed the management function and the use of the 5M's of planning as:

      Men
      Money
      Materials
      Methods
      Machines

Chapter VI described the "personnel cycle" as the managing of the workers to mesh with overall planning.

These three functions can be summarized under a single heading called *Man/Hours Planning*, which is the subject of this chapter.

The use of the management system of "OBJECTIVE-P-O-A to meet objective" can be easily applied to man/hours planning. To do this requires mutual acceptance of a few basic definitions which we will use throughout this phase of study:

1) *Man/Hours* are the result of multiplying the number of employees you have by the number of hours they work daily.

EXAMPLE

Job	No.	Daily Hours Scheduled	Total M/H Daily
Chef	1	8	8
Cooks	3	8 each	24
Service Workers	10	8 each	80
TOTAL	14		112 M/H

Here we have 14 employees and 112 man/hours a day of labor available. A more extensive table and breakdown would take into consideration all personnel and positions, both full and part time, in the unit. The man/hours and payroll cost summary on page 31 in Chapter V (budgeting) makes full use of a man/hours table. In this instance, its purpose is to estimate the payroll cost that can be expected from utilizing the number of man/hours shown. That summary is a good example of total man/hours projections as planned for an operating location, whether for payroll analysis or for man/hours planning.

2) *Man/Hours Planning* is the detailed assignment for each worker of each hour his efforts have been projected as a "Labor Cost" to the unit. In effect, the *WHAT* he will do and *WHEN* he will do it.

A well operated industrial foodservice utilizes the minimum number of man/hours necessary to fill the service requirement. This in turn keeps the "financial need" of the objective at a minimum.

There are various ways to plan the use of the man/hours available to you, but an effective way is the man/hours planning chart, Fig. 15, facing page. This is a common format used by many segments of industry but is especially applicable to the industrial foodservice operation. This chapter will explain in detail how to use such a planning chart as a tool to effectively schedule every man/hour available to you as a manager, or to reduce to a lesser amount the existing number of man/hours scheduled and still fulfill the service requirement.

Objective

Let's go back to the definition of objective as it applies to the use of available man/hours and get a fix on just what must be accomplished.

An industrial foodservice must accomplish three things by the proper use of its available manpower:

1. Produce the necessary menu items in the required amounts.
2. Serve the produced menu to the employees/students/patients of the operating unit.
3. Clean and maintain the facilities that produce the food and provide the service.

All other work performed is subordinate to these three necessary accomplishments.

P-O-A to Achieve Objective

Personnel employed and assigned to the unit as workers range from the manager who does the overall planning—to the chef and cooks who do the production and part of the service—to the dishwasher who does the sanitation and part of the maintenance. Each employee has a maximum number of man/hours available and these must be effectively used. This is the basic plan.

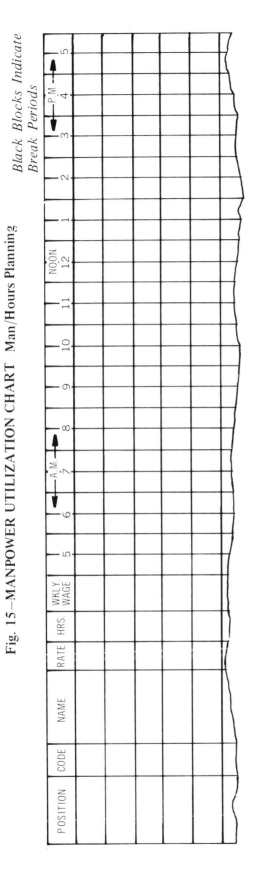

Fig. 15—MANPOWER UTILIZATION CHART   Man/Hours Planning

Black Blocks Indicate Break Periods

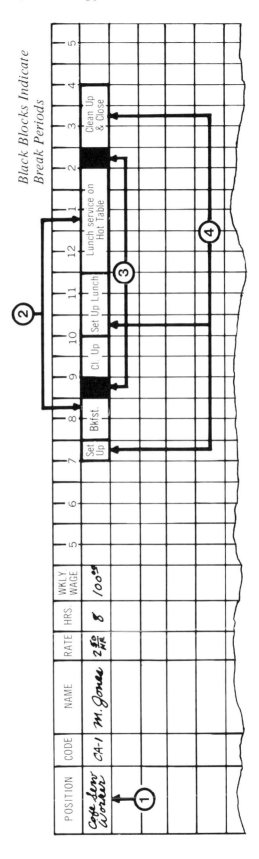

Fig. 16—MANPOWER UTILIZATION CHART   Man/Hours Planning

Black Blocks Indicate Break Periods

Using the man/hours planning chart as a guide, let's take one employee and plan the effective use of his time for one 8-hour day, as an example of man/hours planning.

EMPLOYEE:	Cafeteria Service Worker
SHIFT:	7 A. M. - 4 P. M.
SERVICE:	Breakfast and lunch
	Breakfast short orders
PRODUCTION:	Lunch cakes and pies
	Lunch sandwich station
CLEAN UP:	Cafeteria work station as assigned.

Step One

Place the position title on the man/hours planning chart in the appropriate column on the left side of the chart.

Step Two

Fill in the meal periods that must be served. If breakfast is served from 7:30 to 8:30 A.M., show in a box on the chart that the worker serves breakfast at this hour. If lunch is served from 11:30 to 2:00 P.M., show in a box on the chart that the worker serves lunch at these hours. The meal period assignments are a must as they dictate the use of remaining time.

Step Three

Fill in the break time that the employee will be given. It is typical for foodservice employees to take two short breaks, usually of one-half hour length, rather than a long break of one hour as is normal in office work. These breaks *must* be given and the time period most often used is usually immediately after service of each meal is concluded. At this point, our cafeteria workers' schedule looks like this:

7:00-7:30 A.M.	Open
7:30-8:30 A.M.	Breakfast Service
8:30-9:00 A.M.	Employee Break Period
9:00-11:30 A.M.	Open
11:30-2:00 P.M.	Lunch Service
2:00-2:30 P.M.	Employee Break Period
2:30-4:00 P.M.	Open

The open time of 7:00-7:30 A.M., 9:00-11:30 A.M., and 2:30-4:00 P.M. totals 4½ hours. This must be assigned as production work *before* meal periods and cleanup work *after* meal periods. This obviously results in assigning:

Step Four

7:00-7:30 A.M.	Set up breakfast service station at griddle with eggs, bacon, etc.
9:00-11:30 A.M.	Clean up breakfast station. Cut cakes and pies. Set up lunch station at sandwich board. (Slice meats and cold cuts, tomatoes, etc.)
2:30-4:00 P. M.	Clean up lunch station at sandwich board—store all foods—perform other weekly assigned cleanup chores per schedule.

What remains to be evaluated is the amount of production that can be expected in the 2½ hours between 9:00 and 11:30 A.M., and the amount of cleanup work and/or pre-preparation for tomorrow's production needs, in the 1½ hours between 2:30 and 4:00 P.M. Those 4 hours can be scheduled usefully or wastefully. Your own skill and knowledge of production capacities, equipment available and other related information determine whether these 4 hours will be effective or ineffective hours.

Fig. 16 on page 61 illustrates the way this one position can be placed on the man/hours planning chart and filled in step by step. This should be accomplished for every job in your unit. In exceptionally large units, this can be prepared by department or by shift. Any segment operating independently of other segments can have a chart prepared independently.

CASE HISTORY A

Chart 16A, p. 64 shows man/hours planning for 9 employees of a small unit. This is an actual unit in operation in New York City, servicing a company with 650 employees occupying 7 floors of an office building on Fifth Avenue. The unit provides breakfast and lunch and both a morning and afternoon coffee service using coffee carts. There is no self bussing. The cafeteria seats 140 people. The operation is run by a Chef/Manager. The operation is small and compact, with no executive dining area, or service dining room.

CASE HISTORY B

Man/Hours planning for a larger unit is presented in Fig. 16A, 17, 18 and 19, pp. 64-67. This facility also serves a New York office building operation with breakfast, lunch, and morning and afternoon coffee service by wagons. There is also service for an executive dining area with separate facility and an employee service dining room with waitress service which all employees may use, in addition to the employee cafeteria. Company population is 1800 employees. The facility is extensive, including an on-premise bake shop, full production kitchen, remote storage and receiving areas and remote coffee cart area.

As you can see, there is no comparison in the number of man/hours required to serve the 650 employees of the first case history and the 1800 employees of the second one. The kitchen in operation in the first case history is extremely compact requiring only a Chef/Manager. The operation described in the second case history has an extensive kitchen requiring a chef, cook and utility man, plus bake shop personnel and dining room production personnel.

In both cases, the need for personnel and their related man/hours have been dictated by the service goals of the client company. Man/hours planning has resulted in the use of a minimum number of employees in both locations, but the ratio of 650/9 compared to 1800/43 does not prove this theory. What it does do, however, is to allow the client company in the second case history to fully recognize the "service need" as they have created it and to accept the financial burden of meeting the cost of operations through a heavy annual subsidy far in excess of that required for the operation described in the first case history.

Fig. 16A—MANPOWER UTILIZATION CHART

Black Blocks Indicate Break Periods

Position	Code	Name	Rate	Hours	Weekly Wage
Chef Manager	CHM			40	195.00
Counter Serv.	GF9		3.80	35	133.00
Counter Serv.	GF9		2.85	37	105.45
Counter Serv.	GF9		2.85	37	105.45
Cashier	CA5		2.85	37	105.45
Counter Serv.	GF9		2.99?	35	104.72
Utility	GF9		2.85	35	99.75
Bus Boy	GF9		2.85	35	99.75
UT/Bus Boy	UT		2.02	20	40.40
Total 9 Workers					311 M/H Per Week

Task schedule across time periods (7 through 4):

- **Chef Manager:** Cook Breakfast — Cook Lunch and Supervise Carts — Production-Orders and Bookkeeping
- **Counter Serv.:** Prep. and Serve Breakfast — Prep. Salads and Sand. — Serve on Sand. Board — Clean Up
- **Counter Serv.:** Set Up Coffee Carts — Set Up Counter — Counter Service — Set Up and Take Cart
- **Counter Serv.:** Set Up and Take Cart — Set Up Counter — Counter Service — Set Up and Take Cart
- **Cashier:** Set Up and Take Cart — Check Cash — Cashier — Set Up and Take Cart
- **Counter Serv.:** Breakfast Prep. & Serve — Set Up Counter — Counter Service — Gen. Clean
- **Utility:** Wash. Break. — Dishes — Dish Washer — General Cleaning / Gen. Clean
- **Bus Boy:** Breakfast Prep. & Bus Boy — Set Up Dining Area — Bus Boy
- **UT/Bus Boy:** Pot Washer / Bus Boy — General Cleaning

Black Blocks Indicate Break Periods

Fig. 17—MANPOWER UTILIZATION CHART

Position	Code	Name	Rate	Hours	Weekly Wage	5	6	7	8	9	10	11	12	1	2	3	4	5
Manager	FSM			8	200.00				Breakfast Supervision	■	Supervision of Food Preparation and Luncheon Service			■	Supervise Cash Controls		
Asst. Mgr.	AFS			8	155.00				Supervise Receiving	■	Check Food Preparation. Quality and Luncheon Service			■	Ordering and Sanitation		
Exec. Chef	CH			8	200.00		Supervise Production of All Foods			■	Production and Cooking For Lunch			■			
Cafeteria Supervisor	SUI			8	150.00			Supervise Cold Food Production		■	Cold Food Production and Assists in Pantry			■	Area Sanitation		
STD./Coffee Supervisor	SU2		2.750	8	110.00				Chk "A"	■	Sends Wagons and Check In; Sends Splies & Inventory; Wagon Set up			■	Sends & Checks in Wagons; Verify Receipts		
Sanitation Supervisor	SU3		2.375	8	95.00				Bkfst. Set Up	■	Supervises Sanitation in Dish Room. Cafeteria and Service Dining Room			■	Supervises Final Clean Up of Unit		
Hostess Supervisor	HO		4.200	5	105.00						Supervise Set Up; Supervise Dining Rm & Exec. D.R. Service			■	Clean Up		
Baker	BA		4.400	8	176.00		Bakes Breakfast & A.M. Coffee Run Pastries, etc.			■	Finishes Today's Production & Begins Tomorrow's Work; Equipment Clean Up			■			
Cook	CO		3.900	8	156.00		Hot Food Production			■	Cook For All Hot Food Areas			■			
Short Order Cook	SO		2.450	8	98.00		Sets Up Griddle; Cooks Bkfst & Food for Bkfst. To order			■	Slices Meats & Cheeses; Cooks To Order for Lunch; Clean Up			■			
Kitchen Man	KM		2.450	8	98.00				Assists in Receiving	■	Preparation & Cooking of Food for Chef; Supply Steam Table; Kitchen Clean up			■			
Pot Washer	PW		2.450	8	98.00			Washes Pots & Pans & Aids Chef		■	Washes Pots & Pans; Removes Trays for Cleaning; Cleans Area & General Utility			■			
Exec. Waitress	EW1		4.150	5	103.75						Set Up Dng. Rm.	■	Mixes Drinks and Serves Luncheons to Executives				
Exec. Waitress	EW2		2.950	5	73.75						Set Up Dng. Rm.	■	Mixes Drinks and Serves Luncheons to Executives				
Exec. Waitress	EW3		3.150	5.5	86.63						Set Up Dng. Rm.	■	Mixes Drinks and Serves Luncheons to Executives; Clean Up				
Waitress	W1		2.850	4	57.00						Sets Up Dining Room and Waits on Customers						
Waitress	W2		2.850	4	57.00						Sets Up Dining Room and Waits on Customers						
Waitress	W3		2.850	4	57.00						Sets Up Dining Room and Waits on Customers						

Fig. 18–MANPOWER UTILIZATION CHART

Black Blocks Indicate Break Periods

Position	Code	Name	Rate	Hours	Weekly Wage	Activities (across time periods)
Waitress	W4		2.900	4	58.00	Sets Up Dining Room and Waits on Customers
Waitress	W5		2.850	6.5	92.63	Coffee Cart to 44th Flr. Set Up; Dining Rm & Waiting on Customers: C.C. to 44th Flr.
Bus Boy	BB		2.850	6.5	92.63	Cold Food Preparation for Dining Rm; Dining Rm Set Up; Bussing and Clean Up in Dining Room
Clerk	CL		2.500	8	100.00	Checks Invoices; Clerical Duties as Prescribed; Supervises Cashiers and Monies
Cashier	CA1		2.600	8	104.00	Breakfast Register; Clerical Work: "A" Level Coffee Changers; Luncheon Register No. 2; "A" Level Coffee Changers
Cashier	CA2		2.600	4.5	58.50	Reconcile & Make Deposit; Luncheon Register No.1
Asst. Steward	ST2		2.450	8	98.00	Prepares Coffee for Coffee Run; Receiving and Cleans Urns: Prepares Coffee for Coffee Run; Breaks Down Carts, Clean up
Beverage Man	BM		2.400	8	96.00	Prepare and Set Up for Bkfst. Bev.; Service Special Parties: Prepare, Set Up & Maintain Silver Stations for Lunch: Clean Euipment
Counter Coffee	CC1		2.400	8	96.00	Assists Coffee Cart Set Up: Takes Wagon to 43rd and 18th Floor: Dish Runner; Takes Wagon to 43rd & 18th Flr. Cafe. Clean Up
Counter Coffee	CC2		2.400	8	96.00	Salad Preparation; Takes Wagon to 4th Floor; Serves Steam Table; Takes Wagon to 4th Floor
Counter Coffee	CC3		2.350	8	94.00	Fruit Preparation: Takes Wagon to 20th Floor: Pantry; Takes Wagon to 20th Floor
Counter Coffee	CC4		2.400	8	96.00	Assists Coffee for Coffee Run: Takes Wagon to 19th; Service Steam Table: Takes Wagon to 19th Floor: Clean Up
Counter Coffee	CC5		2.400	8	96.00	Small Salads; Takes Wagon to 10th and 11th Floors Service Steam Table; Takes Wagon to 10, 11: Clean Up
Counter Coffee	CC6		2.350	8	94.00	Assist Coffee Cart Set Up; Take Wagon to 5th & 2nd Floors; Dish Room: Takes Wagon to 5th & 2nd Floor
Counter Coffee	CC7		2.350	8	94.00	Assist Coffee Cart Set Up: Take Wagon to 16th & 17th Flr.; Works at Sandwich Counter: Takes Wagon to 16th & 17th Flr.
Counter Coffee	CC8		2.400	8	96.00	Assist Coffee Cart Set up: Takes Wagon to 4th Floor: Serves on Steam Table; Takes Wagon to 4th Floor
Counter Coffee	CC9		2.350	8	94.00	Assist Coffee Cart Set Up: Takes Wagon to 11th & 12th Flr.; Serves on Steam Table: Takes Wagon to 11th & 12th Floor
Counter Coffee	CC10		2.350	8	94.00	Brings up Stores: Takes Wagon to 5th Floor & "C" Level; Puts Away Stock: Takes Wagon to 5th Floor & "C" Level

Time periods across top: 5, 6, 7, 8, 9, 10, 11, 12, 1, 2, 3, 4, 5

Fig.19–MANPOWER UTILIZATION CHART

Black Blocks Indicate Break Periods

Position	Code	Name	Rate	Hours		Duties
Pantry	PA1		2.400	8	96.00	Breakfast Counter Set Up / Cold Plate Set Up; Sandwich Station No. 1 / Condiment Stands
Pantry	PA2		2.400	8	96.00	Washes Produce & Prep. Salads / Cold Food Preparation; Operates Sandwich Stn. & Griddle for Din. Rm. / Cleans Up Area
Pantry	PA3		2.350	8	94.00	Prepares Fruit-Bkfst & Lunch / Prepares Spreads, Pies & Cakes Maintains Cold Plates / Cleans Up Area
Utility	UT1		2.275	8	91.00	Garbage Room / Cleans Tables, Etc. / Dish Room Station No. 1; Collects Garbage and Takes to "A" Level
Utility	UT2		2.225	8	89.00	Cleans Exec. Pan. / Cleans Equip. & Kitchen Floor / Dish Room Station No.5; Sweeps & Mops And Cafeteria; Garbage Helper
Utility	UT3		2.225	8	89.00	Dish Room / Cleans Dish Rm. / Dish Room Station No. 3; Cleans Bake Shop and Kitchen Area
Utility	UT4		2.275	8	91.00	Cleans Bath & Off. / Sweeps & Mops Cafeteria / Dish Room Station No.2; Cleans Dish Room and Machine.
Total	43 employees					

Let us now take another approach and plan the required man/hours on a total basis for a location rather than for a single employee. The objective set is the need to produce and serve the required number of meals and clean and maintain the premises. In addition, the administrative services of production, ordering, personnel and other such functions must be accomplished to support the objective.

The point of departure is to assess the maximum number of service points that must be staffed at one time and try to operate with as few people above this amount as possible and preferably with no more than the number set.

EXAMPLE

Lunch is usually the heaviest meal period. Case History A above has need for the following lunch stations to serve the cafeteria:

Sandwich Board	1
Hot Food Service	1
Beverage Service	1
Cold Food Service	1
Bus Boy	1
Cashier	1
Dish Room	2
Griddle	1
Total	9

These same 9 personnel are scheduled to accomplish all other service and cleanup functions within the confines of one shift's work schedule.

In scheduling their man/hours, first place all workers on their assigned stations for the lunch period, which in this case is 11:30-1:45. Next, evaluate all other services to be performed. In this case, they amount to servicing 3 coffee carts, twice daily, from 9:15-10:15 in the morning and from 2:30-3:30 in the afternoon. In addition, breakfast is served from 8:00-9:00 A.M.

Man/hours must be found on the chart to place 3 workers on the carts and allow 30 minutes set-up time and 15 minutes breakdown and clean-up time for each cart. This now sets a morning coffee cart need from 8:45-10:30 and an afternoon cart need from 2:00-3:45 for 3 workers. To accomplish this, the bus boy, beverage service worker and cashier are assigned as coffee cart workers and their schedule looks like this:

8:45-10:30	Coffee Cart Service
10:30-11:00	Break period
11:30- 1:45	Lunch Service
1:45- 2:15	Break Period
2:15- 3:45	Coffee Cart Service

All other times for these employees are open; and their starting and quitting times can be determined as seems best.

Once times to meet the service need and the break periods are scheduled, production, cleaning and maintenance work can be filled in to round out the work day. In this case history, these 3 workers are assigned such production chores as making coffee for the wagons, cutting cakes and pies, plating desserts, setting up the cafeteria counter, cleaning cafeteria equipment and sweeping and mopping floors. The cashier is also assigned some administrative duties to assist the chef/manager.

The remaining 6 positions are "man/hour" planned in the same fashion and the total package is put together.

This is a simple case history covering an operation needing few employees but it is extremely well planned with the number of man/hours utilized to accomplish the objective kept to the bare minimum. More complex operations require more extensive planning but utilize the same principle.

In the case of a multi-shift manufacturing plant, each shift could be planned in the same manner as Case History A and then integrated into an overall plan. Administrative duties should be consolidated on the day shift which should also take care of the evening and night shifts. Production chores are usually consolidated on one shift and items left so the other two shifts need only to heat, slice, portion, etc. and serve, thereby saving duplication of production man/hours. It is not unusual to have workers on short shifts, when the dishmachine is not operating, scrape and stack soiled dishes to be washed by the next shift when the dishmachine is in operation. All these methods consume or save total man/hours and, therefore, consume or save total payroll dollars.

In a large college where multiple facilities are operated, each location must have its man/hours planned as a separate entity but the operation will be tied together by the man/hours expended by an administrative staff, in similar fashion to the multi-shift planning in a plant.

In a hospital, each department (i.e. production, diet kitchen, tray assembly, utility, etc.) must have its man/hours planned and the whole tied together by an administrative staff as described.

In all cases, the breakdown of man/hours, their graphic description on a planning chart and reviewing results for the total entity, rather than as individual job functions, is the key.

I have not provided detailed information in this presentation on production man/hours or sanitation and maintenance, but these are equally important areas.

Production man/hours are now an extremely varied figure as today's industrial foodservice kitchen rarely produces a full menu from soup stock to dessert. Most industrial kitchens make extensive use of convenience foods, soup and sauce bases and prepared baked goods and desserts. It is difficult to provide yardsticks that will prove accurate in operating practice as to how many cooks, salad workers, etc. it takes to prepare food for 100, 500 or 1,000 meals. The planning of the necessary production man/hours depends on the management skill of the foodservice manager in evaluating the ability of his staff, the available equipment and the extensiveness of his menu.

As for sanitation and maintenance, Chapter XIII discusses in detail how to plan an effective program to achieve maximum results from minimum labor.

A guiding rule written by a famous consultant and known as Parkinson's Law is "Work expands to fill the time allotted." If you assign one less worker to a group than you feel is enough to accomplish the job, you may often find that the group accomplishes the work load just the same. Large production kitchens, dish rooms and area cleaning are work situations where this may be feasible. If you will think of:

MEN–MAN/HOURS–SERVICE NEED

as a single composite picture, man/hours planning will become easy and effective. Continually keep in mind that man/hours must fill the "service need," but in doing so they can create the "financial need" of the operation. Unless you can defend the need for every man/hour you have scheduled, you are likely to have difficulty in obtaining the subsidy necessary to operate your location effectively.

Remember, OBJECTIVE.....P-O-A to meet the objective. Fig. 19A on page 71 graphically shows how the man/hours planning chart is the organization tool for manpower planning. Apply man/hours planning as the key ingredient to *Men* and you are well on your way to a successful plan.

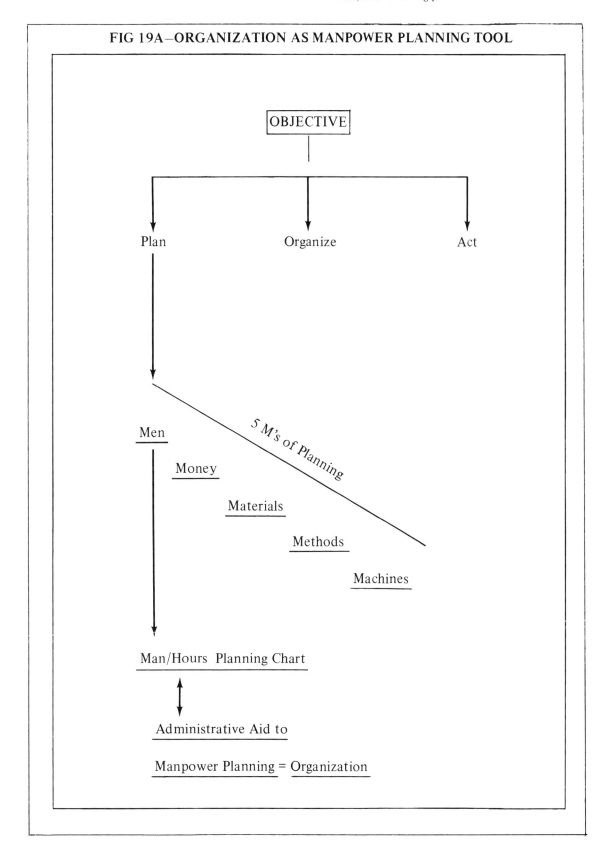

FIG 19A–ORGANIZATION AS MANPOWER PLANNING TOOL

VIII: Establishing a Cost Control System

There are numerous books on the subject of cost control in the foodservice industry and little more can be added to what has already been written. Relating the principles as stated in those books and applying them to industrial foodservice management is essential to successful management.

Cost control is merely keeping track of things. Knowing *where* you have *what* you have at all times, through some easily administered system, is the essence of cost control. The "things" to keep track of are those that cost money. Primarily, this consists of food, labor and cash. You may feel it unusual to list "cash" as one of the three major categories of cost control, but money is as much a commodity in a foodservice operation as a pound of meat or a man/hour.

Over 85% of the cost problems of an industrial foodservice occur in one or all of these three categories. Tight cost control systems that keep food, labor and cash under control usually have a "spillover" effect and control the remaining 15% of the operation's cost problems involving paper goods, laundry, cleaning supplies, etc.

Let's look at each one of the three major categories individually and outline a cost control system that can assist the manager in achieving his operating budget.

Food Cost Control

I have established, as a principle of the process of food cost control for industrial foodservice, what I term *Warner's Law*. This is shown as: $\$ \longrightarrow FOOD \longrightarrow \$\$\$$. Translated, this is read as "Money to food to *more* money."

This law covers seven basic steps, requiring administrative effort and imaginative management, that lead to food cost control.

The flow of money to food to money as it appears in the unit operation is graphically illustrated in Fig. 20 on the facing page. As illustrated, Warner's Law provides an orderly evaluation of the path taken by money as it is *invested* in food and eventually converted back to *more* money. The amount of the increased return must match the food cost goals of the individual unit operation and, ultimately, result in a predictable profit sufficient to allow the

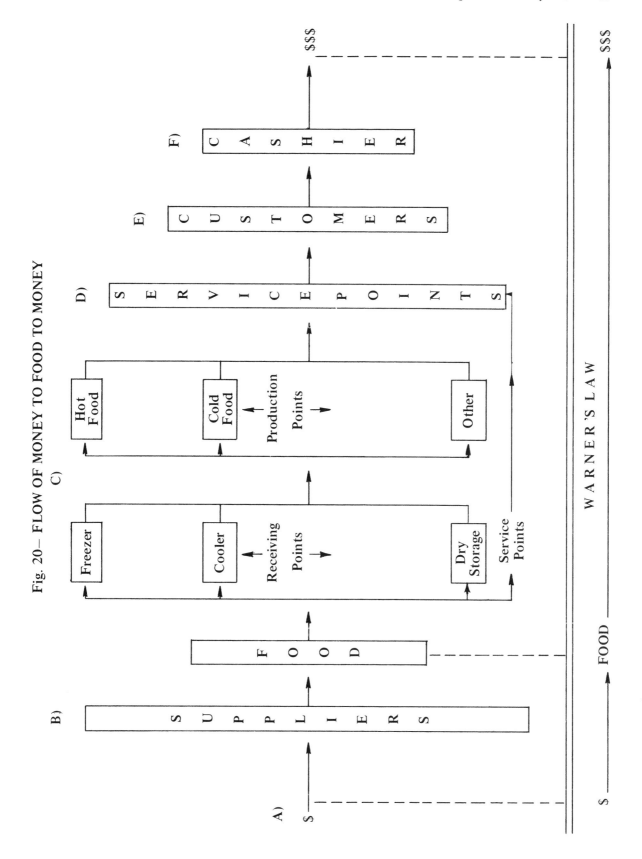

Fig. 20 – FLOW OF MONEY TO FOOD TO MONEY

continuation of the business. This flow can be described as follows:

a)   Investment money is supplied by the company.

b)   This money is "traded" to suppliers for foodstuffs (and other supplies). The investment dollar is now in "soft" goods (food), easily perishable, rather than in "hard" cash, easily redeemable.

c)   The food received is stored at storage points or points of service, where it is held pending production or sale.

d)   Food is moved from storage points, via production processes, to points of service and made available for sale.

e)   Customers are served the end products at the point of service and the sale is consummated.

f)   The customer pays the cashier, and $———▸FOOD———▸$$$ is complete. "Soft" goods now have been returned to "hard" cash.

The ability of a manager to administer the control of this sequence of events effectively will bring success in achieving food cost targets. Lack of an efficient system to control this flow will result in reversal of Warner's Law to "$$$———▸Food———▸$," or "Money to food to *less* money," causing high food costs and resulting in operating losses.

The Seven Basic Steps to Food Cost Control

There are seven basic administrative steps to the effective control of food costs for all industrial foodservice operations. These must be followed and controlled to keep Warner's Law from reversing with resulting excessive food cost ratios that preclude desired budget achievement.

These steps are:

Step One	*Predict* food production requirements.
Step Two	*Order* those requirements systematically.
Step Three	*Receive* those materials properly, check and store them.
Step Four	*Produce* items to be sold.
Step Five	*Sell* the results of production.
Step Six	*Record* the resulting sales information.
Step Seven	*Analyze* the results and *Predict* again.

These seven basic steps, properly planned, effected and administratively controlled, will provide a food cost control system to suit the needs of all four of the areas of industrial feeding.

Analysis of Each Step

Step One—Predict

No goal can be achieved unless it can be defined. In order to supply materials to fill the menu needs, a *prediction* of what is expected to be sold must be made. Future "unit" sales can be predicted by analyzing past "unit" sales. To accomplish this, the "past" must provide a fact gathering system capable of analysis. A fact gathering system consists of cycle menus, sales breakdown information about "unit" sales and similar data. Equipment needed or methods that will assist in fact gathering might be cash registers which give breakdowns; use of denominators; check marks on a pad of paper or beans in a jar. Sophisticated or simple, a fact gathering system must exist.

A "unit" sale is an entree, a piece of pie, a salad or any other measurable "unit" of the menu. *Predicting* requires the necessary information about past "unit" sales to allow a fairly accurate projection of future "unit" sales where the same menu is offered.   An administrative control form or *Production Sheet* must be designed to suit the needs of the operation, its menu format and other criteria. This *Production Sheet* is used both as a recording device for *Predictions* and as a communication device to control *Production.*

Cycling of menus is discussed in Chapter XI in considerable detail so will not be dealt with further here.

Production sheets used for predicting needs vary with the nature of the operation. Most catering corporations have various forms of their own and the unit manager is instructed in how to use them. Production sheets for hospitals and schools differ from those for plants and factories, but basically all provide the same information. A good production sheet provides space to list past sales history, present production, amount produced and amount sold, when the item ran out (if it did) plus space for comments. Fig. 21, p. 76 reproduces an actual form now in use by "a foodservice management company servicing a midtown office building client with 3,000 office type employees." This location is very similar to the one described in Case History No. 1 for the Urban Office Building.

Breaking down unit sales is most effectively handled by a cash register similar to that used by a super-market food store. Other register models on the market allow the breakdown of 20 or more menu items and still more sophisticated equipment exists that allows the breakdown and counting of every item on the customer's tray. These extremely sophisticated machines also require extremely skilled operators and have proven to be impractical in most cases.

Sales information by major "units" of the menu is a must. Some means of accomplishing this must be established. The seventh step, *Analyze*, can only be accomplished if a system of recording "unit" sales exists. Without analysis, predictions cannot be made. Without sales information, analysis cannot be done.

Step Two—Ordering

Ordering is not purchasing. Purchasing is *selecting* vendors and evaluating prices. Ordering is *deciding* how much to purchase. *Ordering* decisions are based on *Production* requirements evaluated in the *Predicting* process.

After "units" of expected sales are predicted, orders required to fill production needs are evaluated. These orders can be filled either from an existing inventory or by purchase from a supplier. This necessitates knowing what is available in inventory before deciding what must be supplied from an outside source. Controlled inventories are a prerequisite to correct ordering. Some form of administrative procedure must be established to effect this control. Such administrative procedure requires daily, weekly or some other periodic record-keeping via effective inventory and order forms suitable to the products that must be handled.

Here again, the catering corporations all have their own system of inventory and order sheets. You should become familiar with various types of ordering sheets and inventory systems. No one system is better than another, except as it is varied to apply in a specific instance. The good unit operator adapts the various inventory/ordering systems he has seen or used to the needs of his specific situation and prepares a set of sheets that meets his specific

Fig. 21–PRODUCTION SHEET

NAME OF CORPORATION

Cycle	Day	Date	Weather
Expected Customers	Help		Total Expected

PRODUCTION SHEET

ITEM	AVERAGE SALES LAST 3 PERIODS	PREDICTION			TOTAL PROD.	SALES			COMMENT TIME OUT

Fig. 22–WEEKLY INVENTORY ORDER SHEET

Unit No.

Items	Unit Pack	Inv. / Ord.	Unit Price	Total	Inv. / Ord.	Unit Price	Total	Inv. / Ord.	Unit Price	Total	Inv. / Ord.	Unit Price	Total

LIST HERE ALL ITEMS REQUIRED FOR YOUR UNIT

Date (×4)

Fig. 23—DAILY STOCK AND ORDER—WEEKLY INVENTORY SHEET

UNIT NO.   W/E

ITEMS	MONDAY		TUESDAY		WEDNESDAY		THURSDAY		FRIDAY		INV.	UNIT PR.	TOTAL
	INV.	ORD.	INV.	ORD.	INV.	ORD.	INV.	ORD.	INV.	ORD.			
LIST HERE ALL ITEMS REQUIRED FOR YOUR UNIT													

needs. Sample daily and weekly order sheets have been reproduced in Fig. 22 and 23, pp. 76-78.

> Remember—ordering is deciding how much to purchase. A standard rule is:
>> *Order for production—produce for sale.*
>> *Do not order for inventory.*

A good operator orders only what his production requirements call for and has little or no inventory on hand.

Step Three—Receive (and Store)

Receiving procedures and standards must be clearly established. These must also be communicated down to all persons who may receive merchandise. Purchase specifications to coordinate the quality, size and pack to be received are the primary tool in efficient receiving. The use of scales, proper temperature of refrigeration and freezers, well kept dry storage areas and properly instructed personnel are the remaining tools required to assure correct receiving and storage.

The goal of receiving and storing is to have merchandise available, in *usable condition,* to meet production requirements as predicted and ordered. There is considerable written material that describes in detail the proper methods of receiving and storing. We only want to stress here that it is one of the major points in food cost control.

Step Four—Production

The guide to *production* is the *prediction.* The same administrative control sheet used to *record* the prediction should be used to *effect* production. Production must be controlled to conform to the prediction of expected sales. Over production leads to leftovers and waste. Underproduction leads to early sellouts and customer dissatisfaction. Both are equally troublesome.

Production is not complete until *yield* has been checked at the point it was produced. The results of production are "shipped" to the point of sale via various hot/cold methods. Shipping to the point of sale may be done in a cafeteria steamtable pan, on a coffee wagon, on a waitress tray or in a carryout container. Hospitals ship to the "point of sale" on a portable cart to a remote ward. In all cases, the kitchen is a production factory turning out products for the "retail outlets" and this production must be controlled by the prediction.

In *Step Two—Ordering,* the rule was given to: "Order for production—Produce for sale." Items that are "bulk" prepared (i.e. roast beef, beef stew, etc.) must be prepared in advance of a meal period in the amount required; the production items that are "cooked to order" (i.e. chicken pot pie, frankfurters, vegetables) can be scheduled in batches after checking the point of sale at half hour intervals. Even a batch item such as Roast Beef can be sliced at intervals during the service period.

The ultimate goal of production is to produce the prediction, but a degree of common sense must be applied to the scheduling, with allowance made for last minute sales information. The ultimate goal of the prediction/production cycle is to have the last customer purchase the last remaining item on the cafeteria line and have it be his own choice. Naturally, this is impossible but it still stands as the criterion for prediction/production.

Step Five—Sell

Products produced in the kitchen and "shipped" to the points of service must be merchandised and sold. This "sale" must be controlled to assure "yield" in the service process. Supervision during the selling process must be maintained to assure that correct portion control is effected. All too often the kitchen "ships" 100 portions of an item (such as beef stew), but the cafeteria counter only "sells" 90 portions and runs out. Overportioning and mishandling at the "selling" point are common problems and prime causes for higher food costs. Effective supervision and control over "selling" is imperative, if the results of production are to return a full yield when sold.

Step Six—Record

The primary recorder of sales is the cash register, recording dollar amounts of each sale, summaries of each period (i.e. breakfast, lunch, etc.) and each day. Cash registers used should also break down "unit" sales into as many categories as possible. Other mechanical means (such as denominators) or manual means (such as pad and pencil, beans in a jar, etc.) can be used to supplement a cash register that will not perform all necessary functions. Some means *must* exist to allow the counting of all major cost items. These include entrees, entree salads, number of sandwiches, number of desserts, etc.

In addition, information obtained from inventory sheets and receiving records must also be converted to dollar amounts to allow dollar comparisons to sales. Periodically, preferably weekly, a summary must be made of all information recorded to allow management review. That summary should, at the minimum, advise:

a) Sales by units
b) Sales by dollars
c) Sales by meal categories (i.e. breakfast, lunch, etc.)
d) Sales by food categories (i.e. meat, dairy, etc.)

Records should also advise management of any other additional information that is pertinent to proper cost control.

Step Seven—Analyze

In order to plan for the use of money in ordering, production and selling in the future, an analysis of past business results must be made. This analysis must be made no less often than weekly and always *before* planning future use of investment money, predicting and ordering.

Analysis must be made with intelligence and honesty. Do not "bend" the numbers. The only one fooled will be yourself. After analysis, *Step One* is repeated and the production process takes place all over again.

These are the seven key points to food cost control that make Warner's Law effective. The key effort in the use of this system is methodical, continuous use of the control tools available. While food cost controls are a necessity, they should not duplicate or encumber. Establishing the use of clip boards and filing systems to simplify the seven basic steps is up to each individual manager and requires little more than common sense. Properly planned and followed through, a program of administrative controls over the seven basic steps, utilizing your past experience and education, will take you via Warner's Law to

$$\$ \longrightarrow FOOD \longrightarrow \$\$\$$$

and a successful control system for food cost.

Labor Cost Control

Labor cost results from man/hours expended. This principle applies to the same degree in industrial foodservice as it does in a manufacturing plant. Knowing what tasks are to be performed and how long they should take is the beginning of an effective labor cost control system. A successful manager has developed the ability to prepare a job description, job breakdown and task breakdown. These skills can be obtained from any good book or academic course on the subject. Establishing the number of personnel that are to be employed, their wage rates and the number of hours they will work, was accomplished at the time the budget was prepared. Labor cost control consists of establishing a review system on a weekly basis to assure that the planned budget is working as planned. Some of the more effective ways to accomplish this are:

1)   As a general rule, do not allow overtime. Where a need for overtime exists, determine whether an absent employee's wage will be saved to compensate for it or whether a special occasion sale will provide the additional monies to cover this expenditure.

2)   Where an additional service is requested (such as an additional coffee cart to go to a new area and requiring an additional worker), write an addendum to the budget and present it to management for approval. The time to ask for the additional money is when the additional service is requested.

3)   Review all time cards weekly and initial them before they are allowed to be transferred to the payroll sheets as man/hours. There is no better way to know when your subordinates arrive and depart than to review their time cards.

4)   In general, pay attention to the work schedule and make sure that it meets the original plan on a continuing basis.

In a school or hospital situation, where labor cost is equated on a "per student meal" or "per patient day" basis, fluctuations in meals or patients served can cause a great fluctuation in the "average" cost of labor per meal. Correct budgeting is the necessary answer. Be sure you have the necessary amount of labor as a *fixed cost* but control the man/hours expended to assure that the *fixed cost* is not exceeded.

Cash Control

Warner's Law is written "Money to food to more money." In all cases of cost control, we are talking about the control of money however it is represented. When you look around your kitchen and see a piece of meat, that represents money in the form of food. When you see a dishmachine operator at a machine, that represents money in the form of labor. When you see a dollar bill in the register, that is money in the form of cash. In every case— food, labor or cash—these items represent cost and require the same methodical control.

Methodical cash control means assuring that all cash sales find their way to the bank account of the company and that all cash funds remain in balance. A dollar missing from cash sales is the same as a dollar's worth of food being burned by the cook in production. In both cases the dollar loss increases operating costs. Every operating unit, whether it is company or caterer operated, has a specific cash handling policy and system.

A unit manager should review that system to assure that there are no "holes" in it and then rigidly enforce the rules of the system. Honest people stay honest on their own basic principles of honesty. Dishonest people stay honest through fear of being caught. A "surprise" audit of cash on hand does not upset the honest cashier, but fear of such an inspection will make a dishonest cashier cautious. A few basic rules that when followed allow good cash control are:

1)   Whenever possible, observe cash register practices of the cashier.

2)   Keep good records of amounts of "over" and "short" for each cashier. No cashier should ever be "even." This indicates she worked all day and did not make a single human mistake. This is exceptionally rare as all employees regularly make human errors.

3)   Periodically do a "surprise audit" of a cashier's register and cash box. An excessive overage may indicate the "stockpiling" of money for future removal; an excessive shortage may indicate a "short-term loan" to the cashier.

4)   Keep accurate control of cash deposits in the bank with verified deposit slips.

5)   Establish and maintain regularity in your daily routine of cash control—but periodically do something different in that routine.

Many other items could be added to this list, but these are minimums. Remember, a good system keeps honest people honest *with pride* and keeps dishonest people honest through fear of being caught.

Earlier it was stated that food, labor and cash constitute over 85% of the cost control problems of any unit. The remaining 15%, such as paper goods, cleaning supplies, etc., will fall in line with cost control, if the first 85% are properly controlled.

The proper use of inventory and ordering to a prediction on food, labor and cash carries over to control paper goods and cleaning supplies.

The proper use of supervisory control over your personnel carries over to control your laundry usage.

The proper use of your own management effort to keep people honest, keeps them honest in all categories, not just cash control.

Good cost controls are good management. Good management is P-O-A.

IX: The Weekly Operating Report

The Weekly Report—Tool for Cost Control

Good management and good managers in any field of business develop tools to assist them in controlling operating costs. These controls are usually in the form of reporting documents that advise the operating manager or other executives at periodic intervals of the status of operating costs. The monthly accounting statement, used by all business, is one such report. In most business enterprises, that monthly accounting statement does not provide sufficient in-depth information regarding operating costs to allow management actions to be taken to keep costs under control, so additional reports are prepared by operations personnel more often.

Explanations of Operating Costs

In any business endeavor there are two types of operating costs, *fixed* and *variable*. Some areas of operating costs include a combination of both fixed and variable but, by and large, one of these two definitions can be given to most categories of cost.

Fixed costs are defined as those that remain constant despite increases or decreases in sales. These are often referred to as "overhead costs." Rent in a retail establishment is one such example. If your rent is $12,000 per year, that amount is fixed; it will vary in relation to sales on a percentage basis only as sales increase or decrease.

Variable costs are defined as those that increase or decrease with sales, usually on a direct ratio basis to the sales dollar. In our industry, food cost is the prime example of a variable cost. If sales increase, the dollar cost of food increases. If sales decrease, the dollar cost of food decreases—*but* the ratio of food cost to sales is supposed to remain constant at a "percentage" figure. The common term "food cost" used by all foodservice managers refers to the percentage value of food purchases to sales.

To repeat:

Fixed Costs—remain constant despite sales fluctuation
Variable Costs—fluctuate in direct percentage ratio to sales.

Understanding these two basic definitions is necessary to implement any cost control system.

The Weekly Operating Report

Industrial foodservice utilizes a document called the weekly operating report as the primary reporting tool for cost control. All contract caterers and managed operations use forms developed by the specific food management companies. Most company-operated facilities use some sort of form, usually developed by that company's accounting department. Some locations, foolishly, do not use any system. To successfully achieve his operating budget, an industrial foodservice manager must be skilled both in using an existing system and/or in developing a needed system of his own. In Chapter III the operating goal was established as both financial and to fill a need. To help establish the financial portion of that goal, an operating budget is prepared. To help achieve the budget, a weekly operating report is used as a management cost control tool.

Format of the Weekly Report

Establishing the format of the weekly report so that it provides management with useful information is extremely important. Questions the report must answer are:

> 1) What is my weekly sales and cost picture?
> 2) Are these sales and costs in line with budget projections?
> 3) If out of line, where and in what categories?

All too often reports become too cumbersome and provide an excess of unnecessary information. As a result, they are poorly prepared and ineffectively used. Today's data processing systems provide voluminous reports that provide much more information than is needed.

The form of your location's weekly operating report should follow exactly the format of your annual budget and provide you with information about 1/52nd of that budget's total goal. Let us break down the budget into its major categories and determine the information desired from a weekly report. Refer to page 17 of Chapter II and refer to budget of Case History No. 1, the Urban Office Building Corporation, which we will use as a model.

The first "control point" of the budget is information about sales. Are they holding? Are they increasing? Are they decreasing? Page 17 shows that the sales projection is composed of projected customer count and expected check averages at various meal periods. The weekly report must, therefore, have a space to record daily and summarize weekly these extra pieces of information. Fig. 24, the Sales Breakdown form on the facing page presents an example of how to accomplish this. The form could be used as a separate report but in this instance is required only as part of an overall weekly report in conjunction with various other data.

FIG. 24 — SALES BREAKDOWN

MEAL PERIOD	SAT.	SUN.	MON.	TUES.	WED.	THURS.	FRI.	TOTAL	
TOTAL									
MEAL PERIOD	CUSTOMER COUNT BREAKDOWN								Check Aver.
	SAT.	SUN.	MON.	TUES.	WED.	THURS.	FRI.	TOTAL	
TOTAL									

The second "control point" of the budget is food cost. This is a *variable* cost and is controlled as a ratio to sales expressed in a percentage figure. In the case of the Urban Office Building, the food cost budget is 50% of sales. Sales are reported as described above.

Food cost is composed of some major categories of purchases dictated by the menu variety. A facility such as the Urban Office Building, with its extensive coffee cart service, would have a different "mix" of purchases than a plant using coffee vending for its coffee break service. Nevertheless, major categories of food cost do exist that are common to all food businesses. Various listings are available from commercial accounting firms, books on food cost control and other similar areas, but it is my opinion that these categories in the industrial foodservice field must reflect the individual cost structure of the following menu items:

1) Hot Entrees
2) Cold Foods
3) Coffee Service
4) Dairy Products
5) Baked Goods
6) Storeroom Items

The operator needs to know how much money was spent daily and weekly for merchandise (food) purchased in each of these categories. He also needs to know the percentage ratio of each category individually and all food purchases collectively. In the final analysis, the operator wants to know, "Did I achieve a 50% food cost this week?" He further needs to know *exactly* why he didn't if his food cost was excessive. Fig. 25 on the following page provides a format for collecting such information.

The third "control point" of the budget is labor costs. At budget time, a specific number of personnel were projected at specific labor rates. These two projections, with the addition of related costs for employee benefits, were equated as payroll dollars. The weekly operating report must provide a space to record the amount of payroll dollars spent and some breakdown as to how it was spent. The purpose of the breakdown is to allow future analysis should payroll expenditures be out of line with budget projections. An example of the breakdown of payroll cost reporting is shown in Fig. 26, p. 86.

Fig. 25—FOOD COST BREAKDOWN

DAY	M.F.P.	PRO-DUCE	DAIRY	BAKED GOODS	COFFEE TEA	GRO-CERIES	TOTAL	DAILY FOOD COST
OPENING INVENTORY								
SAT.								
SUN.								
MON.								
TUES.								
WED.								
THURS.								
FRI.								
WEEKLY TOTAL								
LESS CLOSE INVENTORY								
NET USAGE								
TOTAL								
% TO SALES								

Fig. 26— WEEKLY PAYROLL ANALYSIS

CATEGORY	DOLLARS	MAN/HOURS	BUDGET	
			M/H	DOLLARS
REGULAR				
OVERTIME				
VACATION				
SICK PAY				
HOLIDAY				
MEMORIAL				
CASH PAYROLL				
OTHER				
TOTAL				

FIG. 27–DIRECT OPERATING EXPENSES

DAY	PAPER GOODS	CLEAN. SUPPLIES	LAUNDRY	REPLACE-MENTS	OTHER	OTHER	OTHER	TOTAL DIRECT
SAT.								
SUN.								
MON.								
TUES.								
WED.								
THURS.								
FRI.								
WEEKLY TOTAL								
% TO SALES								

FIG. 28–WEEKLY BUDGET SUMMARY & COMPARISON

YEAR TO DATE 　　　　　　　　　　　　　　　　　　WEEK NUMBER _____

	THIS WEEK	%	THIS YEAR	%	BUDGET	%
SALES						
FOOD COST						
SALARIES AND WAGES						
PAYROLL BENEFITS %						
PAPER GOODS						
LAUNDRY						
CLEANING SUPPLIES						
REPAIRS						
REPLACEMENT & EXPEND.						
OFFICE SUPPLIES						
LICENSES						
MISC.						
TELEPHONE						
INSURANCE & TAXES						
RENTAL						
TOTAL COST						
NET PROFIT (LOSS)						

Payroll costs are both *fixed* and *variable*. In most instances, in an industrial foodservice operation, payroll costs are fixed. When a unit has a portion of its work force that fluctuates with the increase or decrease in business, that portion of the payroll is variable. Examples of variable payroll costs are:

1) Waiter/waitress in a service dining room
2) Utility/dishwashers

Most other personnel are required whether sales are up or down, as the service need of the operating goal must still be fulfilled despite increases or decreases in sales.

The fourth "control point" of the weekly report is *direct operating expenses*. These refer to the *controllable* direct expenses only, such as paper goods, cleaning supplies, laundry and replacements. Other *fixed* direct expenses such as insurance and utilities do not require a weekly reporting control. A form for reporting expenditures of this type is shown in Fig. 27, p. 87. This is identical to the method used for reporting food cost by category breakdowns. It is merely a listing of days of the week and the dollar amounts of each purchase—summarized weekly and compared to the sales dollar.

The fifth "control point" is to summarize, in a weekly operating statement, the exact information that appears on the monthly accounting statement and, in effect, prepare a "memo" statement. This should further be summarized as "year to date" information and compared to "year to date" budget goals. Such a statement appears in Fig. 28, p. 87. This shows the weekly statement, and the yearly statement "to date," along with a sub-section of the annual budget "to date."

All five of these control points must be combined into a weekly report for evaluation and analysis by the unit operator. One such report, Fig. 29, is reproduced on pp. 90-91. This particular report was prepared as an "open end" document to allow the operators of many different types of locations to "write-in" the necessary headings for sales categories and statement items. As the operator of a specific installation, such as the Urban Office Building, sales categories are taken from the budget and are written in as shown in Fig. 30 on pp. 92-93. This is an actual copy of a report prepared by the manager of an employee cafeteria located in an urban city. Note that they have modified the cost breakdown portion of the report to suit the needs of their four-week accounting system (EDP by period) and to eliminate the use of opening and closing inventories. In this example, net purchases equal cost percentages.

Proper preparation and timely evaluation of a well-designed weekly operating report is probably the most important budget expense and cost control task performed by a unit manager. I refer to this as Warner's BECON system of control from the initials Budget, Expense, Control. A well thought out and properly effected BECON system can well make the difference between your own personal success or failure as a unit manager.

Evaluating the Weekly Report

The mere gathering of statistical information and summarizing it in a weekly report is of little value, unless the report is intelligently evaluated. Chapter IV described the P-O-A system of management. The weekly operating report is part of the O - *organization*, but the addition of the A - *action* on the part of the unit manager is paramount to its effectiveness and his own success.   The following sequence and system is an effective method of evaluating a weekly operating report.

a) Purchases and Inventories

The food cost section of your report shows the amount of the opening and closing inventories and the daily purchases of each category of food. It also summarizes total purchases and net usage by category, and in total, and provides percentage ratios to sales by category and in total as well.

Each unit must establish its standard norms for the category used in the breakdown of the food cost budget. These will be heavily governed by the sales mix of the menu in your unit.

Once established, sub-headings of budget costs by categories should be used to break down the total food cost. In the case of the Urban Office Building, with a projected food cost of 50% total, sub-categories would look like this:

Meat Fish Poultry	_13.0_ %
Produce	_5.5_ %
Dairy	_9.0_ %
Baked Goods	_11.0_ %
Coffee/Tea	_4.5_ %
Groceries	_7.0_ %
Total	_50._ %

Often the total goal of 50% is achieved although an individual category is out of line to a great degree. The area out of line should be immediately investigated and action taken. Often an incorrect inventory will show a distorted cost percentage for a category.

Many opinions exist on the use of inventories as a weekly control device. My own opinion is that the difference in inventories should only be evaluated once a month and weekly food cost control systems should reflect actual purchases. This encourages minimum purchasing and minimum inventories and, therefore, makes for lower food costs. (This is discussed further as WARNER'S LAW in Chapter VIII.)

A full evaluation of "Did I make my food cost *this week?*" and "If not, why not" must be made. Food is a variable cost. Money spent for food that is not returned as sales is forever lost. This evaluation must be made weekly.

b) Sales Information

Many things affect sales but, primarily, the number of customers and the check average determine the actual result of sales.

Each week a unit manager should evaluate whether or not he has achieved the budget goal of:

1) A specific percentage of participation of population (employees) per meal period.

2) A specific check average per meal period.

If sales are below expectations, an analysis of whether the customer count or the check average is down must be made.

Fig. 29– WEEKLY OPERATING REPORT

UNIT NAME: _____   NO: _____   WEEK ENDING: _____

COST BREAKDOWN												
DAY	M.F.P.	PRO-DUCE	DAIRY	BAKED GOODS	COFFEE TEA	GRO-CERIES	TOTAL	DAILY FOOD COST	Paper Goods	Clean. Supplies	Laun-dry	Equip-ment
Open Inv.												
Sat.												
Sun.												
Mon.												
Tues.												
Wed.												
Thu.												
Fri.												
Weekly Total												
Less Inv.												
Net Usage												
% to Sales												

COMMENTS		Period Sales Summary			WEEKLY PAYROLL ANALYSIS		
						$	Man/Hrs.
	Wk.			Total	REGULAR		
	1				OVERTIME		
	2				VACATION		
	3				SPECIAL		
	4				SICK PAY		
					HOLIDAY		
					MEMORIAL		
					Transfrs.		
					Cash		
					TOTAL	$	M/H
					% TO SALES	%	Budget M/H _____

DIST: ORIG: DIV. OFC.   COPY: DIST. OFC.   COPY: UNIT FILE

Menu Cycle No.: _____

WEEK NUMBER: 1–2–3–4

MEAL PERIOD	SALES BREAKDOWN							
	SAT.	SUN.	MON.	TUES.	WED.	THURS.	FRI.	TOTAL

MEAL PERIOD	CUSTOMER COUNT BREAKDOWN								Check Aver.
	SAT.	SUN.	MON.	TUES.	WED.	THURS.	FRI.	TOTAL	

Summary per client Budget	This Wk.	%	Year to Date	%	WEEK NUMBER _____ BUDGET	%
SALES		100		100		100
FOOD COST						
SALARIES AND WAGES						
PAYROLL BENEFITS %						
PAPER GOODS						
LAUNDRY						
CLEANING SUPPLIES						
REPAIRS						
REPLACEMENT & EXPEND.						
OFFICE SUPPLIES						
LICENSES						
MISC.						
TELEPHONE						
INSURANCE & TAXES						
RENTAL						
Adm. Fee						
TOTAL COST						
NET PROFIT (LOSS)						

UNIT MANAGER'S SIGNATURE: _____

Fig.30—WEEKLY OPERATING REPORT

UNIT NAME: _____ NO: _____ WEEK ENDING: __8-18-72__

				COST BREAKDOWN								
DAY	M.F.P.	PRO-DUCE	DAIRY	BAKED GOODS	COFFEE TEA	GRO-CERIES	TOTAL	DAILY FOOD COST	Paper Goods	Clean. Supplies	Laun-dry	Eq me
Sat.												
Sun.												
Mon. 8/14	308.36	51.39	50.29	65.21	—	—	475.25	85.5%				
Tues. 8/15	—	22.42	41.01	49.39	—	—	128.58	23.%			47.59	
Wed. 8/16	75.20	109.27	111.41	67.65	—	—	363.53	67.7%				
Thu. 8/17	—	20.48	28.33	61.74	92.90	—	203.45	34.6%	122.21			
Fri. 8/18	—	—	39.66	68.03		116.35	224.04	28.7%			3.78	
Weekly Total	383.56	203.56	270.70	312.02	92.90	116.35	1394.85	46.2	122.21	—	51.37	
% To Sales	12.7	6.7	8.9	10.3	3.0	3.8	46.2		4.0		1.7	
Week No. 1-2-3-4	648.36	241.56	454.61	560.68	224.27	472.20	2601.68		301.05	78.43	106.22	164
Total	1031.92	445.12	725.31	872.70	317.17	588.55	3996.53	50.3%	423.46	78.43	157.59	164
% To Sales	13.0	5.6	9.1	11.	4.	7.4	50.3		5.3	.9	2.	2

COMMENTS		Period Sales Summary			WEEKLY PAYROLL ANALYSIS		
Low food cost due to incorrectly computed grocery bill. Sexton requests our holding payment until new bill arrives		Wk.		Total		$	Man/H
		1	2188	2188	REGULAR	1170.40	554.
		2	2728	4916	OVERTIME	3.23	1.0
		3	3016	7932	VACATION		
		4			SPECIAL	20.00	
					SICK PAY		
					HOLIDAY		
					MEMORIAL		
					Trnsfrs.		
					Cash		
					TOTAL	$ 1193.63	555.0
					% TO SALES	39.5 %	Budget

M/H

DIST: ORIG: DIV. OFC. COPY: DIST. OFC.COPY: UNIT FILE

Menu Cycle No.: _I_

WEEK NUMBER: 1 – 2 –③– 4

SALES BREAKDOWN								
MEAL PERIOD	SAT.	SUN.	MON. 8/14	TUES. 8/15	WED. 8/16	THURS. 8/17	FRI. 8/18	TOTAL
Bkfst.			15.42	19.61	23.40	20.13	18.68	97.24
Lunch			379.02	367.91	342.89	394.00	268.95	1752.77
Coffee			161.17	171.51	169.97	173.37	165.94	841.96
Sup.			–	–	–	–	324.50	324.50
Total			555.61	559.03	536.26	587.50	778.07	3016.47

MEAL PERIOD	SAT.	SUN.	MON.	TUES.	WED.	THURS.	FRI.	TOTAL	Check Aver.
CUSTOMER COUNT BREAKDOWN									
Bkfst			64	77	88	76	71	376	.26
Lunch			480	494	433	494	349	2250	.79
Coffee			621	663	648	656	628	3216	.26
Sup.			–	–	–	–	218	218	1.48
Total			1165	1234	1169	1226	1266	6060	.49

Summary per client Budget   WEEK NUMBER 51

	This Wk.	%	Year to Date	%	BUDGET	%
SALES	3016	100	155,710	100	157,835	100
FOOD COST	1395	46.2	78,774	50.5	80495	50.9
SALARIES AND WAGES	1194	39.5	70407	45.2	86377	54.7
PAYROLL BENEFITS %	179	5.9	7912	5.0	9555	6.
PAPER GOODS	122	4.	8796	.5	7988	.5
LAUNDRY	51	.1	2461	1.	2498	1.5
CLEANING SUPPLIES	–		704		1438	.9
REPAIRS						
REPLACEMENT & EXPEND.	–		3127	.4	617	.4
OFFICE SUPPLIES						
LICENSES						
MISC.						
TELEPHONE						
INSURANCE & TAXES	5	.2	42	.5	9807	.6
RENTAL						
Adm. Fee 190	211	7	10898	7	11041	7.
TOTAL COST	3157	104.	183171	117	209815	132.
NET PROFIT (LOSS)	(141)	4.	(27461)	17.	(51980)	32.

UNIT MANAGER'S SIGNATURE: _Mary Jones_

If the customer count is down, an investigation should be made as to whether the employee population is also down and, in that case, whether the percentage ratio of population using the foodservice facility is holding.

If population has not decreased and the customer count is down, something about the operation has become less appealing to customers and they have found an alternate place. No group of employees is truly captive. If your unit is not to their liking, they will manage to find an alternate place to eat.

If sales are down due to lowered check average, analysis must be made of the menu, entree mix, price mix and other such variables.

An awareness of exactly what caused the drop in sales—customer count or check average—will lead to the correct management action to find a solution.

c) Payroll Information
A review of the actual expenditures for payroll versus the budgeted allowance for payroll must be made. If the expenditure is in excess of budget, a further review should be made to decide:

1) Were man/hours in line with budget?
2) Was there unnecessary overtime?
3) Are there extra employees on the payroll?
4) Have any accounting mistakes been made that resulted in incorrect payroll payments? This is usually an easy area to evaluate and take action on. However, payroll abuse in overtime and the use of superfluous employees is common and must be corrected.

d) Other Operating Costs
Paper goods, cleaning supplies and replacements are budgeted as a *variable* cost and related to sales. These must be reviewed to assure that they have not exceeded the allowed variable percentage.

Laundry costs have been budgeted as a fixed cost per employee week, with an allowance per week for kitchen linen. A review and evaluation to assure that your unit did not use an excess of linen should be made weekly.

Laundry management left uncontrolled can easily double the normal laundry costs of an operating unit. This area must be kept under tight review.

e) Summary Information
The summary section of the weekly operating report shows a 1/52nd segment of the annual statement as it was accrued for that week and a year-to-date segment covering what has already occurred. It also shows what should have been achieved for the year-to-date portion of the budget.

A comparison of *ACTUAL* to *BUDGET* on a year-to-date basis must be made, evaluated and acted upon. Any single category out of line with budget projections should evoke immediate action on the part of the unit manager.

Hospitals and Schools
Insofar as the need to report weekly on the expenditures for food, labor and supplies

and to record the income from cash transactions is concerned, both hospitals and schools have the same requirements as an urban office building. However, the need for analyzing of these costs and determining to what to relate them differs to a great degree.

In a school or college, the criteria for judgment is cost per student meal, day or week Sometimes more than one weekly report must be prepared in a college facility to permit this assessment. Where regular cash sales cafeterias and snack bars are operated, the same style of weekly report used in Case History No. 1 will suffice. When the students pay a boarding rate for multiple meals per week and no cash sales are involved, a different summary must be incorporated into the weekly report. The weekly report, Fig. 31 on pp. 96-97 illustrates the way this information can be compiled. Notice that all areas of expenditure are still listed in the same manner but the evaluation relating costs to student meals has been changed.

In a hospital operation, major changes occur in the need to report. It was previously mentioned that much of the cost of hospital services is reimbursed to the hospital by insurance companies, such as Blue Cross Medicare and Medicaid. As a result, cost reporting systems must conform to the overall cost accounting system used by the hospital industry. Here again, the compiling of expenditures (costs) for food, labor and various supplies and services follows the same pattern, but the yardstick for measurement changes. Instead of using relationships such as "ratio to sales," as in the case of food cost in a plant or office building, all costs are expressed in ratio to patient meals or patient days.

Weekly operating reports must, therefore, indicate the cost of the categories, FOOD–LABOR–SUPPLIES, then show the cost of each of these items separately as well as totaled on a per patient meal and per patient day basis. Fig. 32, the weekly report on page 98 is an illustration of a properly filled-in report.

In summary, the weekly operating report is the measuring tool to advise the manager of any facilty–plant, office, school, or hospital–how his operation's performance is measuring up in meeting the annual budget objective.

Fig. 31–SCHOOL FOODSERVICE DIVISION–WEEKLY OPERATING REPORT

UNIT _____

						FOOD COST BREAKDOWN	
DAY	MEAT FISH POULTRY	PRODUCE	DAIRY	BAKED GOODS	GROCERIES	TOTAL FOOD COST	SUPPLIES
SUN.							
MON.							
TUES.							
WED.							
THURS.							
FRI.							
SAT.							
WEEKLY TOTAL							
COST PER MEAL							
TOTAL NUMBER WEEKS							
TOTAL							
COST PER MEAL							

COMMENTS: _____
_____
_____
_____
_____
_____
_____
_____
_____
_____

Menu Cycle _____

WEEK ENDING _____   Week Number 1 — 2 — 3 — 4

MEAL COUNT						SUMMARY			
REGULAR STUDENTS	DAY STUDENTS	FACULTY	OTHER	TOTAL			THIS WEEK	THIS MONTH	THIS YEAR
						Number of Meals			
						Food Cost			
						Food Cost Per Meal			
						Labor Cost			
						Labor Cost Per Meal			
						Supplies Cost			
						Supplies Cost Per Meal			
						Total Cost			
						Total Cost Per Meal			

			SPECIAL EVENTS		
	THIS WEEK	THIS MONTH	THIS YEAR
FOOD			
LABOR			
SUPPLIES			
TOTAL			
NUMBER SERVED			
COST PER MEAL SERVED			

Fig. 32–HOSPITAL FOODSERVICE–WEEKLY OPERATING REPORT

COST BREAKDOWN														
	M.F.P.	DAIRY	BAKED GOODS	COFFEE TEA	GROC.	PRO-DUCE	TOTAL	%	PAPER	CLNG. SUPS.	EQUIP.	TOTAL	%	PATIENT DAYS
Sunday														
Monday														
Tuesday														
Wed'day														
Thurs.														
Friday														
Sat.														
TOTAL														
Net Cost														
Per Day														
% Purch.														

COMMENTS	PAYROLL SUMMARY		
	Dietary:		
	Cafeteria:		
	Overtime:		
	Vacation:		
	Other:		
	SUB TOTAL:		
	% Benefits		
	TOTAL PAYROLL		
	Budget Payroll		

Week Ending   1 2 3 4 5

CAFETERIA SALES BREAKDOWN								
MEAL PERIOD	MON.	TUES.	WED.	THURS.	FRI.	SAT.	SUN.	TOTAL
Breakfast								
Lunch								
Dinner								
Other								
TOTAL								
Aux.								

CAFETERIA CUSTOMER COUNT BREAKDOWN									Check Aver.
	MON.	TUES.	WED.	THURS.	FRI.	SAT.	SUN.	TOTAL	
Break									
Lunch									
Dinner									
Other									
TOTAL									

	This week	This period	Fiscal year	Budget amount
Patient days				
Gross Food				
Less Cafeteria				
Less Aux.transfer				
Less Functions:				
Net Food				
Food cost per Patient Day				
Payroll cost				
Payroll cost Patient Day				
Supplies Cost				
Supplies cost Patient Day				
TOTAL COST				
TOTAL COST PER PATIENT DAY				

Mgr. _____

X: Accounting and the Foodservice Unit Manager

Accounting has been defined as the language of business, and this is a most appropriate definition. "Business," for the purposes of this discussion, is the term used to describe a chain of events that (1) begin with the effort made by an employee to provide a service and (2) require a compensatory wage or, (3) if the process is a retail sale it must culminate in some form of an evaluation to decide how much, if any, profit was made on the sale. Accounting is the "language" used by businessmen to evaluate such activities. Admittedly, this is an oversimplification of the accounting process and function. However, it suffices as a basis for the material covered in this chapter.

As a unit manager of an industrial foodservice facility, you will be held responsible for basic accounting at the unit level. This will include:

1) Cash Handling and Control:

Administrative control and reporting of cash on hand, daily cash sales, bank deposits and similar details.

2) Payroll Procedures:

The reporting of hours worked by each employee and the processing of this information to convert man-hours to payroll dollars.

3) Accounts Payable Processing:

The "logging" of all delivery tickets and/or vendors' invoices to arrange an orderly process for payment of bills.

4) Miscellaneous Matters:

These are similar to the above and may include reviewing and comparing summarized reports and understanding basic accounting regarding credit memos, discounts, etc., that are normally accomplished by a unit manager.

The three primary areas of unit accounting that remain constant throughout all operating locations are: *cash, payroll,* and *accounts payable.*

Use of Data Processing

Almost all areas of business accounting today utilize electronic data processing in one form or another. As a result, the unit manager must have a working knowledge of how EDP (electronic data processing) works in order to accomplish the basic accounting functions required of him in his unit manager's position.

Today every person is familiar with his own Social Security number which identifies his "account" with the Federal Government for Social Security taxes and retirement benefits. He is also quite likely to be familiar with the number of his bank account, charge account or some other account numbers. *These are all identifying account numbers.*

The average person also understands the basic use of a personal check, a sales slip from a retail store or a vendor's delivery ticket.

These are all "source" documents. The basic procedure of EDP is to relate *"source" documents* to *"account" numbers* and process them through mathematical programs; to add them up, take discount payments, prepare summarized accounting statements and other similar procedures necessary to the business for which they are processed. This is done via the computer.

A unit manager prepares these "source" documents and identifying account numbers according to a prescribed procedure, using various forms in accordance with the company's accepted methods. Whether your unit is "caterer operated" or "company operated," the method you will use will be the same as that used by every other unit or department for processing information to be translated by the company's accounting department into the language of everyday business.

Let's take a closer look now at each of the three main areas and observe how they are handled at the unit level.

Cash Handling and Reporting

Cash in an operating unit consists of the cash bank that is *initially provided* and the incoming daily cash sales. A unit manager is responsible for maintaining the balance of the cash bank at all times and for depositing the cash sales daily in a designated bank or with a designated office of the company.

Procedures will change depending on whether you are company or caterer employed. In a "company" operated unit, you will usually prepare a daily cash report similar to that used in a caterer operation but often will not have to prepare a weekly summary.

Fig. 33, pp. 102-103, is an example of a cash reporting form used by the company in Case History I. Fig. 34, p. 104, is another example of a form used by a smaller operation which combines cash reporting with other necessary daily reporting information. Although forms differ, the basic information they account for is the same. Basically, a daily cash report provides the following information to both the unit manager and the accounting department:

1) Information on opening and closing readings for all cash registers in the unit.
2) Statistics on customer count at each register.
3) Summary of cash on hand at the close of the shift on a business day.
4) Summary of the cash bank being retained in the unit.
5) Over/short information on daily cash.
6) Summary of the amount of money from sales being deposited in the bank or left at a designated location.

Many cash reports provide additional information, such as sales by meal period recorded

Fig. 33—CASH REPORTING FORM

DAILY SALES AND CASH REPORT

Prepared By _____   Approved By _____

DATE _____   WEATHER _____

CASH SALES		REGISTER READINGS	GROSS SALES	OVER SHORT	TAX READINGS	NET SALES	CUSTOMERS	CHECK AVERAGE
Register 1 *LOBBY*	Closing							
	Opening							
	Net							
Register 1 Breakfast	Closing							
	Opening							
	Net							
Register 1 Lunch	Closing							
	Opening							
	Net							
Register II *LUNCH*	Closing							
	Opening							
	Net							
Register III Lunch	Closing							
	Opening							
	Net							
Register IV Lunch	Closing							
	Opening							
	Net							
Register *A.M.* COFFEE SERVICE	Closing							
	Opening							
	Net							
Register V Coffee Service	Closing							
	Opening							

Net

Register V — Cash Sales — Closing / Opening / Net

SUB-TOTAL — Deposit

Register V — Charge Sales — Closing / Opening / Net

Outside Sales

TOTAL SALES — Deposit

TRANSFER COSTS:
35th and 50th Floor

Special Functions

TOTAL TRANSFER COSTS

SUMMARY	DEBITS	CREDITS
Cash		
Cafeteria Sales		
Accounts Receivable		
Breakfast		
A.M. Coffee Run + LOBBY		
P.M. Coffee Run		
Cash Sales (D.R.)		
Sales Tax (Cash)		
Charge Sales (D.R.)		
Sales Tax (Charge)		
Outside Sales		
Outside Sales Tax		
TOTAL		

REMARKS:

misc. Key I
II
III
IV

Fig. 34–DAILY RECAPITULATION

Manager's
Signature _____ Day & Date _____ Location: _____

BREAKFAST, LUNCH, WAGONS, ETC.		Register	Amount Rung Up	Over	Short	Net Cash Sales	MDSE. REC'D			
							VENDOR		ITEM	AMOUNT
1	CUR PREV									
2	CUR PREV									
3	CUR PREV									
4	CUR PREV									
5	CUR PREV									
6	CUR PREV									
7										
8										
9										
10										
11										
12										

TOTAL CASH SALES

CHARGE SALES COLLECTED:
DATE OF CHARGE   FROM WHOM

MDSE. OR CONTAINERS RETURNED

MISC. INCOME:

CASH DEPOSITED (DATE   19   )

SUMMARY
CHARGE SALES: (Indicate to Whom Charged)   AMT.

COMMENTS: (PLEASE INDICATE SHUTDOWNS
FOR VACATIONS, HOLIDAYS, ETC., OR ANY
OTHER CAUSE FOR SALES VARIATIONS.)

TOTAL CHARGE SALES

CASH SALES

TOTAL

DEDUCT–SALES TAX

SALES FOR DAY

by using multiple opening and closing readings on the cash register; check averages determined by dividing meal period sales by meal period customer counts; summaries of petty cash funds; summaries of "payouts" (cash purchases of materials) or any other information that management wishes summarized and reported daily. This information is really supplementary to the basic need of reporting your cash position daily. Basically, a cash report provides the information described in points one through six above.

Payroll Procedures

Almost all caterer-operated facilities of major corporations now use EDP to computerize their payroll operations. Company-operated facilities use the payroll systems in force for the main portion of their business and these are also usually computerized.

Some small operations still utilize "hand payroll" accounting methods, but a large portion of these use computer services now available to the small businessman via banks, insurance companies or computer service bureaus. It is more likely that as a unit manager you will prepare a source document for a computer payroll rather than a payroll form for a manually prepared system. Therefore, only the computer method of payroll accounting at the unit level will be described and discussed here.

The Source Document

Each employee in your unit is given a payroll identification number at the time of hiring. To supply this number, the unit manager fills out a prescribed form (source document) prior to the new employee's first week of work. This request form often encompasses other information desired by the company for the personnel or other departments that need specific data about any new employee that has been hired. One such form used by the Interstate-United Corporation is known as an "801 Form." Almost all such forms derive their identity from the number given to the form. This payroll source data must supply the following information about the new employee:
1) Name
2) Number of dependents
3) Social Security number
4) A Federal Form W-4 used for withholding tax purposes.

Requests for other information, such as the new employee's age, eligibility for employee benefits, etc., are often added. Directions for preparing the form are usually available as a "procedure" and are either issued as part of the form or are contained in a procedure manual. Fig. 35, p. 106, is an 801 form. The payroll procedure in the Interstate-United Manual on preparing the payroll section of the 801 form is excerpted on pp. 107-108. These are typical of all EDP payroll systems, although the specifics of the form and the procedure will vary from company to company.

The Reporting Form

After the source document for each new employee has been completed, his name is placed on a reporting form, which is usually referred to as the payroll sheet. This form will contain the pre-printed names of all employees of a unit down a left side column with various headings across the top of the page above other columns as illustrated in Fig. 36, pp. 110-111. Note the provisions for reporting the regular hours, overtime hours, vacation wages, special payments and other similar information about each employee.

Fig. 35—PERSONNEL AND PAYROLL AUTHORIZATION

PLEASE DO NOT FILL IN SHADED AREAS

PLEASE PRINT

UNIT OR COMPANY NAME

PERSONNEL AND PAYROLL AUTHORIZATION

AS OF

UNIT NO.

EMPLOYEE NO.   DEPT. NO.

NEW HIRE 01 - 03	REHIRE 01	TERMINATE 999	TRANSFER 998	RATE CHANGE 03	OTHER

EMPLOYEE NAME (LAST, FIRST)   SOCIAL SECURITY NO.   DATE OF BIRTH   DATE OF HIRE

MONTH DAY YEAR   MONTH DAY YEAR

44

REASON HIRED

REASON FOR HIRING
N-NEW JOB OPENING
R-REPLACED TERMINATED EMPLOYEE
T-TEMPORARY REPLACEMENT

WORK STATUS
1-FULL
2-PART
3-STUD
6-TEMP

SEX
1-MALE
2-FEM.

RACE

MARITAL STATUS
1-MARR
2-SING
3-HEAD

WEEK HIRED

OVER TIME
1-YES
2-NO

ADDR. ON CHECK
1-YES
2-NO

STATE LV IN

CITY LV IN

DATE OF REHIRE
MONTH DAY YEAR

REAS

CHECK ONE
0-NEW
1-CHANGE   01

STREET ADDRESS   CITY

STATE   ZIP CODE   EXCEPTION DATA FOR TAXES   EXCEPTION FIELDS ARE TO BE USED ONLY IF EMPLOYEE DOES NOT WORK OR LIVE (PA & OH) IN SAME STATE OR CITY THE UNIT IS LOCATED IN.

STATE   CITY   ALL TAX

CHECK ONE
0-NEW
1-CHANGE   02

HOURLY RATE   WEEKLY SALARY   EXEMPTIONS FED. STATE CITY   ACCOUNT NO.   UNION LOCAL   MEAL ALLOW.   LNDRY.   ENTER % OF INCREASE FOR SALARIED _____ % EMPLOYEES ONLY.

JOB TITLE

REASON FOR INCREASE CODES
M-MERIT   L-LABOR CONTRACT
P-PROMOTION   O-OTHER
R-REVIEW   N-MERIT/PROMOTION

ENTER ONE

REA   DATE INCREASE EFFECT   DATE NEXT REVIEW   JOB CODE   HRLY./SAL.   ENTER PROPER CODE FOR EITHER NEW HIRES OR RATE CHANGES

MONTH DAY YEAR   MONTH DAY YEAR

H-HOUR
S-SAL.

JOB GRADE

CHECK ONE
0-NEW
1-CHANGE   03

LAST DAY WORKED   DATE TERMINATED   REA   WOULD YOU REHIRE EMPLOYEE?
Y-YES
N-NO

HAS ALL COMPANY PROPERTY (CREDIT CARDS, VEHICLES, CASH ADVANCES, MONEY BANKS, UNIFORMS, TOOLS, ETC.) BEEN RETURNED.
YES   NO (EXPLAIN ON REVERSE SIDE)

NOTICE GIVEN BY EMPLOYEE   YES ___ WKS.

EMPLOYEE SIGNATURE (VOLUNTARY RESIGN)

MONTH DAY YEAR   MONTH DAY YEAR

999

TRANSFER FROM/TO   REA

TYPE OF TRANSFER CODES
L - LATERAL   T - TRAINING
P - PROMOTION
R - REQUEST

DATE EFFECTIVE   NEW CORP. NO.   NEW ACCOUNT NUMBER   NEW STATE   UNION ELIGIBILITY DATE
MONTH DAY YEAR
1-USE ORIGINAL OR REHIRE
2-USE TRANSFER DATE

998

PREV. HR RATE   PREV. SALARY   REA.   EFFECTIVE DATE   SAL/HR   JOB CD   BOND PRICE   CO-OWNER OR BENEFICIARY

INS. PLAN   AMOUNT PAID BY EMPLOYEE   LIFE INS. VOLUME   ADDL. LIFE INS. VOLUME   A.D. & D. VOLUME   SICK BENEFIT VOLUME   PAI VOLUME   BENEFICIARY FOR INSURANCE

LTD INS. COVERAGE   BENEFICIARY FOR PROFIT SHARING   DATE ON PLAN

DEDUCTION	AMOUNT	DEDUCTION	AMOUNT	DEDUCTION	AMOUNT	DEDUCTION	AMOUNT

REASONS FOR TERMINATION (ENTER CODE IN SECTION 999)

A TEMPORARY LAY-OFF
B PERMANENT LAY-OFF-TERMINATED
C STRIKE AT CLIENTS LOCATION-WORK AVAILABLE
D STRIKE AT CLIENTS LOCATION-NO WORK AVAILABLE
E THIS EMPLOYEE ON STRIKE
F FAILED TO REPORT FOR WORK
G FAILED TO RETURN FROM LEAVE OF ABSENCE
H UNSATISFACTORY PERFORMANCE
I INSUBORDINATION

J CHRONIC OR EXCESSIVE ABSENTEEISM
K EXCESSIVE TARDINESS
L PERSONAL MISCONDUCT
M VIOLATION OF COMPANY-POLICY-RULES-PRODECURES
O ACCEPT ANOTHER POSITION
P MEDICAL-TERMINATION
Q DISSATISFACTION WITH PRESENT POSITION
R LACK OF TRANSPORTATION

S RETURN TO SCHOOL
T LEAVING JOB MARKET OR CITY
U RETIREMENT-VOLUNTARY
V RETIREMENT-COMPULSORY
W LEAVE OF ABSENCE-PERSONAL
X LEAVE OF ABSENCE-MEDICAL OR PREGNANCY
Y LEAVE OF ABSENCE-MILITARY (LONG TERM)
Z DEATH

REMARKS (USE BACK OF FORM IF MORE SPACE REQUIRED)

REQUESTED BY   DATE   APPROVED BY   DATE   APPROVED BY   DATE   SIGNATURES

FORM 801 (1/71)

PREPARATION OF FORM 801 FOR NEW HIRES (EXHIBIT B)

(*)   This information must be completed or the employee will *not* be paid.

    1. Check New Hire Block at Top of Form and complete sections 01-03 of the 801 as follows:

(*)   2. Enter Unit Number for proper identification of the location.

    3. Enter Department number—complete where applicable.

(*)   4. Enter Employee Name. Use one of the following methods to enter a name:

        a) Jones, John A.

        b) Jones, Jr., John A.

        NOTE: Comma must be shown after last name.

(*)   5. Enter Social Security Number.

(*)   6. Enter Date of Birth.

(*)   7. Enter Date of Hire.

(*)   8. Enter the appropriate code for Reason Hired.

(*)   9. Work Status. Enter the appropriate code in the area provided.

        Full—   Full Time Employee

        Part—   Part Time Employee

        Stud—   Student

        Temp—   Temporary Employee

(*) 10. Enter Sex Code.

(*) 11. Enter Marital Status. Enter the appropriate code to determine the proper income taxes to be deducted from the employee's pay.

        MARR-   Married

        SING—   Single

        HEAD—   Head of Household

(*) 12. Enter Overtime Code—Is the employee eligible for overtime pay? Enter Code 1 if yes, 2 if no.

(*) 13. Enter Address on Check Code. Whenever it is necessary for an employee to receive a check at his home address, i.e. a Salesman who is generally not in the office, enter a Code "1," otherwise enter "2." If code "1" is used the 801 must be approved by the next higher level of management.

(*) 14. Enter Street Address of employee's place of residence. It may be entered:

        a) 1234 South Anystreet

        b) 1234 S. Anystreet

(*) 15. Enter the City of employee's place of residence.

(*) 16. Enter State Abbreviation. See Exhibit 1 for the appropriate abbreviation for each state to be entered in the space provided.

    17. Enter the Zip Code.

(*) 18. Enter Hourly Rate or Weekly Salary. Fill in whichever one is applicable to the employee being hired. Hourly rate can be entered to 3 decimal place for cents.

        i.e. 1.350 or 1.335

    For salaried personnel enter the weekly amount in dollars and cents:

        i.e. 125.35

    NOTE: Enter the salary or hourly rate aligned with the decimal point preprinted in each area of the form.

(*) 19. Enter the Federal, State and City exemptions. This information should be entered in accordance with the Federal W-4 and the appropriate state and/or local tax exemption certificates that are to be filled out, signed by the employee and attached to the Corporate Office copy of the 801.

    20. Enter Union Local Number. If an employee must join a union at some later date in order to remain on the job, enter the appropriate union local number on the 801. This does not replace the union enrollment card needed to start deducting dues and initiation fees when the appropriate wait periods have been satisfied.

    21. Enter meal allowance where applicable. If the employee is to be charged for FICA tax purposes for the standard meal allowance that has been set up for the entire unit by state regulations, leave area blank. If the employee is to be charged for a rate other than the standard rate, enter this rate in meal allowance. Should the employee be exempt from all meal allowances where there is a standard rate, enter "9999."

If meal allowances do not apply to the unit, do not make any entry at all.

Examples: A=   Standard rate is .25 cents a day and employee is to be taxed on standard, leave blank.

B=   Standard is .25 a day and employee is to be taxed on .40 a day, enter "0040."

C=   Standard is .25 and employee is exempt from tax, enter "9999."

22. Enter Laundry Allowances—If employee is eligible to receive an allowance enter any applicable cents amount from (01 cents) to (99 cents). This amount will then be calculated as amount times hours worked to arrive at the allowance.

EXAMPLE: .05 cents times 40 hours = $2.00 allowance.

NOTE: If allowance is a weekly amount, submit information directly to the Corporate Payroll Department and do not make any entry on the 801.

(*) 23. Enter Job Code—See Exhibit J for proper codes.

(*) 24. Enter Hourly/Salaried Code. This code indicates whether the employee is hourly or salaried. It must be used in conjunction with the hourly rate or weekly salary fields (see No. 18). If an hourly rate was entered, the letter "H" must also be entered. If a weekly salary is entered, the letter "S" must be used.

(*) 25. Check the "O-New" Box in section 01, 02 and 03. This indicates that this information is for a new hire.

A unit manager must learn how to translate the information from each employee's time card to the payroll sheet just as the key punch operator must learn to "read" it into the computer. Here again, a prescribed "procedure" is provided as part of a procedure manual available to the unit manager for reference. The reporting form acts as a source document for payroll information that is put into the computer by the key punch operator.

Accounts Payable Function

Each day your unit will receive merchandise and/or services. These are usually accompanied by a delivery ticket, receipt or other form that identifies what you have received and how much it is supposed to cost. This is the "source" document from which the accounts payable department of your company or the organization you work for, pays the suppliers for that material or the company for the service that you received.

Whether your employer's accounting system is manual or computerized, these documents are processed in basically the same way:

Under a manual system, receiving tickets are summarized on a form specified by the company and, though they may differ in appearance, all forms summarize the information on the receiving ticket, identifying:

1) Vendor's name
2) Amount of the invoice
3) Identifying number on the invoice
4) Account you wish to charge this invoice to (i.e. food, paper, supplies, etc.)

An example of this type of form known as a Daily Record of Invoices is reproduced in Fig. 37, p. 114.

Under a computerized system, some additional information must be reported about each invoice since it is now a "source" document being given to a key punch operator to convert into computer language. This information usually includes:

1) Vendor's identifying number (Each vendor you use has an identifying number in your computer)

2) Amount of any discounts or rebates the invoice may be allowed
3) Date of the invoice
4) Account code of the charge
5) Other specialized information desired by the individual company

As a unit manager you will be expected to fill out the necessary source document to summarize the information required by the key punch operator. Again, a procedure will have been written and will appear as part of an "accounts payable" section of a procedure manual. A form, Fig. 38, used by the Interstate-United Corp. as well as an excerpt of part of the procedure devised for preparing the form appears on pp. 115-117. This shows how that company prepares an accounts payable procedure to be used by their unit managers to prepare the required source document to initiate the accounts payable function.

Summary Reporting

Whether your unit has a manual or computer accounting system, an operating statement will be prepared once a month and used by all levels of management to assess the performance of the foodservice department whether it is a company-operated location, or the foodservice unit of a caterer-operated location. The levels of management that will see this report go from the unit manager on up to the president of the company as accounting is the language common to all levels of management.

It is the management responsibility of a unit manager to assure that the information on this statement is correct. All too often a manager is prone to feel that, since he has forwarded correct information, the statement should be correct. Human beings process all of a unit's accounting work, whether it is computerized or not, and human beings make mistakes. A wise unit manager verifies the information on his monthly statement by comparing it with his own administrative reports covering all material submitted for processing into the statement.

Fig. 36–PAYROLL TIME SHEET

WEEKLY PAYROLL

_____   _____   _____
Unit Name   Unit No.   Dept. No.

EMPLOYEE NAME	JOB CODE	EMPLOYEE NO.	HOURS						
			REGULAR	OVER-TIME	DOUBLE TIME	VACA-TION	HOLI-DAY	SICK OR PER-SONAL	OTHER
			14	18	21	24	28	31	35
ENTER TOTALS ON LAST PAGE ONLY									
PAYROLL DEPARTMENT USE ONLY									

ORIGINAL COPY TO CORPORATE OFFICE, DUPLICATE COPY TO BE RETAINED.

FOR COMPLETE INSTRUCTIONS ON USE OF FORM SEE REVERSE SIDE.   PREPARED BY _____

PAGE _____ OF _____

TIME SHEET   FOR WEEK ENDING _____

DAYS		No. Of WEEKS PAY	TIPS REPORTED FORM 812 NOT TO BE PAID	OTHER EARNINGS-DOLLARS					REMARKS SECTION
PAID	ACCUM. H.O. USE ONLY			GRAT./ COMMIS.	SHIFT-JOB RATE DIFF. OR PREM.	MISC. AMOUNT	C	VACATION	
39		42	44	49	55	60	67	68	
									ENTER ALL HOURS IN TENTHS
	✕								

_____   _____   _____

DATE   APPROVED BY   DATE

ENTER IN RED OR CIRCLE AMOUNTS TO BE SUBTRACTED EXCEPT FOR MISC. SEE REVERSE SIDE.

INSTRUCTIONS FOR PREPARATION OF THE WEEKLY PAYROLL TIME SHEET

Regular and overtime hours must be entered on the time sheet in tenths of an hour according to the following table:

Minutes	Tenths of an Hour	Minutes	Tenths of an Hour
0 to 5	.0	30 to 35	.5
6 to 11	.1	36 to 41	.6
12 to 17	.2	42 to 47	.7
18 to 23	.3	48 to 53	.8
24 to 29	.4	54 to 59	.9

A.   Check the pay period ending date to insure that the latest time sheet is used.

B.   Enter the number of pages. If one page, show page 1 of 1. If 3 pages, show page 1 of 3 on the first page, page 2 of 3 on the second page, etc.

C.   *Regular Hours*—Enter the total regular hours to be paid for each hourly employee. Circle the word "PAY" in the "DON'T PAY ***PAY***SALARIED" message, but do not show regular hours for salaried employees. If, for some reason a salaried employee does not work any hours and is to receive no pay, circle the word "DON'T" in the message under regular hours and explain in the remarks section. If a salaried employee is to receive more or less than one week's pay, enter the amount to be added to or subtracted from his weekly salary in the miscellaneous earnings column with the appropriate code (see section P).

D.   *Overtime Hours to be Paid at Time-and-a-Half*—Enter the number of hours *actually worked.* Do not enter overtime hours for salaried employees.

E.   *Double Time Hours*—Enter the number of overtime hours to be paid at double the employee's regular rate.

F.   *Vacation Hours*—Enter the number of vacation hours to be paid at the straight time hourly rate. In the Remarks section indicate the vacation period as follows: e. g. 2 weeks vacation due from June 6 through June 17.

G.   *Holiday Hours*—Enter the number of holiday hours to be paid for at the straight time hourly rate. In addition, enter the number of hours worked in the regular or overtime hours column if an employee is to be paid at the regular or overtime rate for working on a paid holiday.

H.   *Sick or Personal Time Off*—Enter the number of hours not worked due to sick or personal reasons for which the employee is being paid. These hours will be computed at the straight time hourly rate.

I.   *Other Hours*—Enter the number of hours the employee is being paid for at the straight time rate not provided for in the order columns. An entry in this column must be fully explained in the Remarks section. An example might be an adjustment or correction to the number of hours reported on a previous time sheet. Hours which are to be subtracted must be circled or entered in red.

J.   *Days Paid*—This column will be used for employees whose vacations are based on the number of days paid for (maximum of 5 days per week). When the employee is to receive vacation pay, circle or enter in red the number of days to be subtracted from the total of accumulated days. For example, a vending employee requesting two week's vacation pay in addition to his regular week's pay would have a negative 250 (25 x 10) for the vacation taken and a plus 5 for the week worked. Thus a minus 245 is entered in the days paid column.

At any time the particular number of days printed by the computer on the time sheet represents days paid for and is used to compute eligible vacation days.

Where days worked are used to determine vacation for employees covered by union contract, the terms of the contract will apply.

K. *Days Accumulated*—The accumulated days will be printed in this column for units using days worked or paid for in determining vacations. Errors in this column can be corrected with a plus or minus entry in the days worked/paid column. The "Days Accumulated" column is not to be filled in by the unit.

L. *Number of Weeks Pay*—Enter the total number of weeks to be paid for hourly and salaried employees if the employee is to be paid for more than one (1) week.

M. *Tips Reported*—(Not to be Paid)—Enter the amount of tips reported by the employee on Form 812.

N. *Gratuities or Commissions*—Enter gratuities to be paid as wages resulting from employees serving banquets and similar functions. Also enter commissions due to certain vending employees.

O. *Shift or Job Rate Differential or Premium*—This refers to hours worked at a rate other than the employee's regular rate. The amount entered is the number of hours worked times the difference in rates. For example, an employee working the night shift may be entitled to an additional 10¢ per hour. If he worked 24 hours on the night shift, the hours would be included in the regular hours column and $2.40 entered in the shift premium column.

P. *Miscellaneous*—Enter all other earnings and adjustments not provided for in the other columns. A detailed description or explanation must be entered in the Remarks section. Examples of earnings which would be considered miscellaneous are:

More or less than one week's pay for a salaried employee except for vacation pay advances covered in J.
Adjustments

Sunday standby, usually a fixed amount.
Service Call pay, usually a fixed amount.

Miscellaneous Codes (Use the appropriate code)

D-Deduction From Salary or Earnings
E-Extra Day Worked—Salaried Emp.
H-Holiday Pay—Salaried only
L-Laundry Allowance

O-Over-time Salaried Emp.
R-Retroactive Pay
S-Sick or Personal—Salaried only
No Code—Any other miscellaneous additions to earnings

Q. *Vacation*—Enter the dollar amount to be paid employees for vacation. If the employee is hourly rated but does not receive vacation pay at his regular hourly rate please calculate the amount to be paid and enter the figure in this column. If a dollar amount is entered for an hourly rated employee in this column, there must not be any hours entered in the vacation hours column for that employee.

R. If the employee's name does not appear on the pre-printed list, enter his name and hours worked after the last pre-printed name. An 801 form must be prepared to add an employee to the unit's payroll.

S. If the employee has terminated, cross out his name and write in the word "terminated." An 801 form must be prepared to terminate an employee.

T. Enter the totals of all columns on the last page of the time sheet. Do not include hours worked by salaried employees in these totals.

U. The person who prepares the time sheet must sign it; the unit manager must approve it.

V. Forward the original DP-1A to the Corporate Office payroll department and retain the duplicate for your file.

Fig. 37 — DAILY RECORD OF INVOICES

PREPARED BY: DAY: DATE:

INVOICE DATE	INVOICE NO.	VENDORS NAME	M.F.P.	PROD-UCE	DAIRY	BAKED GOODS	COFFEE TEA	GROCER-IES	PAPER GOODS	CLEAN. SUPPLY	LAUN-DRY	EQUIP.	COMMENTS
		TOTAL											

ACCOUNTS PAYABLE PROCESSING INDUSTRIAL FOOD UNITS

I. **SCOPE**
   This procedure outlines the processing requirements for accounts payable documents for those units of Interstate United Corporation classified as foodservice units.

II. **EXHIBITS**
   Exhibit A (1 & 2) - Form P-23, Accounts Payable Document Envelope, Food Units. (see pp.116 and 117).

   Exhibit B - Form F-1, Weekly Summary of Purchases and Expenses.

   Exhibit C - Accounts Payable Department Envelope, Form E-132.

III. **GENERAL**
   In order to generate accurate cost information for each food unit, all data relating to receipt of merchandise or services must be directed to the Corporate Office Accounts Payable Department at the conclusion of each week.

   The individual responsible for processing accounts payable information at the unit must assemble receiving information, by vendor, on all charges for the week. This is accomplished by daily filing of invoices (or delivery tickets) into separate accounts payable document envelopes (Exhibit A-1) by vendor. At the end of each week, all invoice charges from a given vendor should then be within a single envelope.

   All vendors are to be instructed to render a priced and extended invoice at the time the merchandise is delivered. If the vendor <u>does not</u> do this, it is the responsibility of the unit manager to determine the price of the item(s) and extend the invoice accordingly. All invoices and delivery tickets **must be** priced and extended before being directed to the Corporate Office.

IV. **PROCEDURE**
   A. Enter the following information in the area of the envelope as indicated on Exhibit A-1 before mailing the envelopes to the Corporate Office for processing.

   1. Enter unit number.
   2. Enter Vendor number - Refer to Vendor master list, by unit.
   3. Enter Vendor name.
   4. Check block if new Vendor number is not available.
   5. Check block to indicate when payment should be made. If you check:
      a. Immediate—Payment will be made immediately upon reaching the Corporate Office.
      b. 30 days—Payment will be made 30 days from invoice date.
   6. Verify and check that:
      a. <u>Goods</u> or merchandise was received.
      b. <u>Unit Cost</u> is what you agreed to pay vendor for merchandise.
      c. Extensions - Unit price times quantity equals line amount and the sum of all lines agrees to what is shown on invoice.
   7. Enter the signature of the person preparing the envelope.
   8. Enter authorized manager's initials.
   9. Enter unit name.
   10. Enter <u>cash discount</u> percentage (%) only.
   11. Enter <u>trade discount</u> percentage (%) only.
   12 Enter invoice date.
   13. Enter invoice number if available.
   14. Enter account code number as follows:

CODE   DESCRIPTION
2020   Vend/Other—this account is to be used for vending machines operated by the manual unit and for "over-the-counter" items not a regular food product, such as aspirins, cigarettes, gift shop items, etc.

Fig. 38–SUMMARY OF INVOICE INFORMATION

A-1

UNIT NO.	VENDOR NO.	VENDOR NAME

☐ CHECK IF NEW VENDOR

PAYMENT (Check One)	VERIFY AND CHECK ALL THREE	PREPARED BY (Signature)
1. ☐ IMMEDIATE 2. ☐ 30 DAYS	☐ GOODS RECEIVED ☐ UNIT PRICE O.K. ☐ EXTENSIONS O.K.	

MANAGERS INITIALS	UNIT NAME	CASH DISCOUNT %	TRADE DISCOUNT %
		%	%

INVOICE DATE	INVOICE NUMBER	ACCOUNT CODE	GROSS INVOICE AMT. (CIRCLE CREDITS)	CHECK IF INV. ALTERED

GROSS INVOICE AMOUNT	
NET INVOICE AMOUNT	

A-2

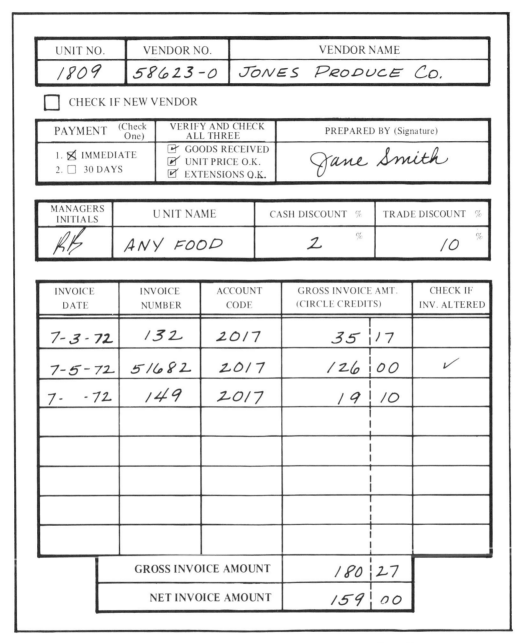

UNIT NO.	VENDOR NO.	VENDOR NAME
1809	58623-0	JONES PRODUCE CO.

☐ CHECK IF NEW VENDOR

PAYMENT (Check One)	VERIFY AND CHECK ALL THREE	PREPARED BY (Signature)
1. ☒ IMMEDIATE 2. ☐ 30 DAYS	☑ GOODS RECEIVED ☑ UNIT PRICE O.K. ☑ EXTENSIONS O.K.	*Jane Smith*

MANAGERS INITIALS	UNIT NAME	CASH DISCOUNT %	TRADE DISCOUNT %
RB	ANY FOOD	2 %	10 %

INVOICE DATE	INVOICE NUMBER	ACCOUNT CODE	GROSS INVOICE AMT. (CIRCLE CREDITS)		CHECK IF INV. ALTERED
7-3-72	132	2017	35	17	
7-5-72	51682	2017	126	00	✓
7- -72	149	2017	19	10	
	GROSS INVOICE AMOUNT		180	27	
	NET INVOICE AMOUNT		159	00	

TRADE   180.27   CASH
180.27   -18.03   162.24
.10%   162.24   .02%
18.0270   -3.24   3.2448
=   159.00   =
18.03   3.24

XI: Menu Management and Administration

The purpose of this chapter is to explain the use of menu planning as it relates to menu administration and menu management. The terms "menu administration" and "menu management" are not commonly used, but they should be. Let's align them with the P-O-A principle discussed in Chapter IV, Understanding Management, and define them further.

P—Plan

Menu planning is the detail work involved in laying out the menu format and inserting the items—from appetizers to desserts, that have been selected to be offered. The plan must suit the desired objective as to variety and cost.

O—Organization

The *administrative* practices required to accomplish orderly menu planning include filing, research, and analysis. Organization is the structure that holds the plan together.

A—Act

Menu management is the action taken to assure that the organizational methods are followed and that the menu plan is continually reviewed, controlled and altered as necessary to achieve the operating goals of the unit.

If P-O-A is carried out, the objective will be achieved.

In industrial foodservice, with its four different types of operation, the operating goal can differ from one area to another. Good menu management is an essential part of overall management toward achieving the operations objectives.

The Menu

What is a menu? Exactly, what does it do for your business? Any retail business establishes "product lines" which it sells to the public. A department store separates its men's wear sales from its women's wear sales. An automobile agency usually sells both small and large models of the same car. A hardware store carries paints and wallpaper as well as hand tools. These are all examples of the "product lines" of those retailers.

In the industrial foodservice location, the menu establishes the product lines being offered and these product lines, in turn, establish the production requirements for the kitchen. In addition, the menu establishes the "sales mix" of products sold which affect the food cost percentage. This is an important part of menu management.

Planning—The Menu Format

The first step in menu planning for an industrial operation is to establish the *format* for the menu. How many appetizers, soups, entrees, salads, desserts and beverages will be offered for sale at each meal period? What variance will be allowed from the basic format? Unlike a commercial operation that is open to the public, an industrial foodservice usually provides a menu to suit a specific group.

EXAMPLE

a) factory workers
b) office workers
c) students
d) patients in a hospital
e) elderly in a nursing home. . .and similar groups.

Menu formats must be geared to suit the need of each individual operation or unit. In some instances, the menu format will be limited by the equipment available to produce the menu, by display space on the cafeteria line available to serve items on the menu and, on some occasions, by union pressure on the employer to provide specific varieties of foods to their members.

Menu formats should have as a "base" the broadest segment of the service need and "add on" the various other requirements of the location. The "base" is usually the main cafeteria menu (with the exception of hospitals) with dining room, coffee cart and other menus being the "add-ons."

Case History No. 1—The Office Building

The Urban Office Building, cited in Case History No. 1, has 2,000 employees and provides the services of morning and afternoon coffee carts, an employee cafeteria and an executive guest dining room. The menu format for the cafeteria is the "base" of all planning, with the coffee carts and dining rooms acting as "add-ons" to that base.

The cafeteria menu uses the following format:

Appetizers	*Entrees*	*Sandwiches*
3 juices	1 broiled meat or fish	11 varieties, made to order
2 other	1 stew or extended dish	2 ready made at special
	or casserole	prices
Soups		
1 heavy	*Vegetables*	*Desserts*
1 light	2 potatoes	2 two crust pies
	1 starch	1 single crust pie
Salads	2 other	1 cake
1 large entree		2 specials
1 small entree	*Beverage*	1 pudding
3 side salads	Assorted hot and cold	1 gelatin
		1 fruit
		1 ice cream

With this format as the base, dining room menus "add on" to the production need and create a waitress service menu.

EXAMPLE

The dining room would utilize the entrees of the cafeteria, combine them with some of the vegetable and potato items. . .add an appetizer or soup and dessert and could then serve a club luncheon, waitress style.

A third special item would be added to the entrees in the dining room that would not be available in the cafeteria.

Grilled items (hamburgers, etc.) would be added as part of the dining room menu, but would not be available on the cafeteria line.   All other soups, salads, desserts and beverages would be the same as the cafeteria.

As previously stated, the cafeteria menu is the "base" and additional items are "added on" that are more applicable to a waitress service dining room.

Coffee carts provide a special requirement all their own and their menu affects the bread/ roll/pastry area of the overall menu format. Morning cart service in the New York area, where the operation covered by this case history is located, features a variety of rolls and breakfast pastries. Leftover rolls from this service are placed at sandwich stations and usually are sold as part of the sandwich line. Leftover breakfast pastry items rarely sell at lunch time and need to be incorporated into other secondary items, i.e. bread/cabinet puddings, etc. Afternoon coffee cart service utilizes snack type pastries, usually wrapped and with a multi-day shelf life. These items have very little effect on the remainder of the menu format, but are treated as a separate entity.

When it is all put together, the overall format and plan now look like this:

	CAFETERIA	DINING ROOM	COFFEE CARTS
Appetizers	3 juice ⟶		Orange juice at AM
	2 other ⟶		Other juice at PM
Soups	1 heavy ⟶		
	1 light ⟶		
Entrees	1 broiled meat or fish ⟶		
	1 other ⟶	plus 1 special dish	
Vegetable	2 potatoes ⟶	1 plus French fries	
	1 starch ⟶		
	2 other ⟶		
Salads	1 large entree ⟶		
	1 small entree ⟶	plus 1 special platter	
	3 side ⟶		
Sandwiches	10 varieties ⟶	plus grilled items	
Desserts	Pies ⟶		
	Cakes ⟶		fresh fruit at PM
	Puddings, etc. ⟶		
Beverages	Assorted ⟶		coffee, tea, milk

Wherever possible, multi-use of the same base items utilized on the cafeteria format is desired.

Case History No. 2—The Manufacturing Plant

In the manufacturing plant, with multi-shift operations, some additional planning of the menu format is required. A three-shift plant usually has the cafeteria service open for a short period prior to each shift's arrival and for the mid-meal period of each shift. Cart service for "break" periods has become almost extinct in plants and factories, with vending machines usually providing this service. A typical 24-hour meal service schedule would look like this:

1st Shift: 12 Midnight—8 A. M.

Pre-shift service, 11:00 P.M. to 12:00 midnight menu would consist primarily of beverages and snacks. The average worker is not interested in heavy food and only those who have traveled a considerable distance are interested in anything at all.

Mid-shift service, for one hour around 3 A.M., is a combination of breakfast and lunch. Different workers develop different eating habits when working an all night shift and make extra demands on the food service. Usually one entree is served and the remaining menu is sandwich and short order, with some breakfast items.

2nd Shift: Plant—8 A. M.—4 P. M.

        Office—9 A. M.—5 P. M.

This shift combines plant and office employees and, therefore, it commingles tastes and service needs. In addition, some departing first shift employees will "snack" or eat before starting a long trip home.

The cafeteria usually opens around 7 A.M. to service the 8 A.M. shift and remains open to service the arriving 9 A.M. shift. A typical breakfast menu is offered with emphasis on local taste preferences.

Mid-shift lunch begins around 11:00 for plant workers who usually break in shifts in 15 to 20 minute sequence. Depending on the type of manufacturing done at the plant, lunch breaks for different departments are scheduled so they do not adversely affect the production line process. In some industries that have "continuous flow" manufacturing processes, a runner picks up food and takes it to the plant worker; the steel industry is one that requires this kind of service. In each operation, the production need of the plant establishes the lunch break schedule.

Office workers in the same plant may break for lunch at intervals between 12 and 1:30 P. M.

The menu format must satisfy both the factory worker and the office worker at the lunch meal. This creates the need to satisfy two separate consumer groups at the same time from the same menu format. This requires ingenuity and imagination on the part of the foodservice manager, as each group usually complains that the menu is oriented too much toward the other group.

3rd Shift: 4 P. M.—12 Midnight

This group is usually made up of 90% plant employees plus a small percentage of clerical/office personnel. A pre-shift snack service is often provided that is identical to the pre-shift service for the first shift.

Mid-shift meal period is a repetition of lunch with less emphasis on the office worker demand. Here again, as with the first shift, employees have different habits of eating and desire short order or full meal service depending on personal choice.

As you review the foregoing three shift meals, you can see that the second shift lunch period requires the heaviest and most extensive meal. Therefore, the lunch menu becomes the "base" format and other meal periods "add on" from that point (with the exception of breakfast). If a foreman's or service dining room were to exist, it would usually be for lunch only and would vary in the same way as the dining room in Case History No. 1.

Considering all the variables stated, a menu format for this case history would look like Fig. 39, facing page.

With this format, the second shift lunch is planned with all other shift/periods "added on."

Case History No. 3–Hospitals

Menus in hospitals are a special part of patient care. Unlike the office building, plant or school, the "guest" in a hospital is there by chance and not choice. What he is provided to eat can have a positive or adverse effect on his total well-being and must be given great consideration.

While preparation of the full menu is usually the responsibility of a trained therapeutic dietitian, the planning of the format is still the responsibility of the foodservice director or manager and follows the same system as the other areas of industrial feeding. A basic format is established, with add-ons acting as extensions to the format.

In most hospitals, various diets are outlined in a diet manual. This diet manual is a scientifically balanced set of menus geared to meet the therapeutic needs of any of the diets prescribed for a patient by his doctor. In addition, a regular or "house" diet is served to all other patients who are not on special prescribed diets. This "house" diet is usually the "base" format from which the "add-ons" of special diets should be extended.

The house diet may be a selective menu (allowing the patient a choice from a multi-entree menu) or a non-selective menu (in effect, boarding house style). In either instance, it should serve as the base for the menu format. A hospital may have many or few children (pediatrics) or older people (geriatrics) which will also have a strong effect on the menu plan. It is impossible to generalize about hospital menu planning except to state that it is always a part of total health planning. Planning the menus requires skill and knowledge far above the planning of most industrial foodservice menus and should be done by a qualified dietitian.

Case History No. 4–College/School

Schools and colleges have varied foodservice schedules and it is impossible to generalize regarding menu format. While some schools operate a "boarding" menu with typical breakfast, lunch and dinner service, others operate a cafeteria style menu on a 5-day basis only. In addition, most schools have snack bars, soda fountains and vending available which many students use at all times. Menu "format" in a college/school situation must be developed based on the need of the unit.

While this explanation is less detailed than those in Case Histories No. 1 and No. 2 that appear in the preceding pages, the same philosophy of developing a "base" format with "add-ons" can and should be developed. A close study of Case Histories No. 1 and 2 will allow the manager to develop the principles of a menu format plan and adapt them to the specific college/school need.

Fig 39–MENU FORMAT–MANUFACTURING PLANT

	2nd SHIFT LUNCH	3rd SHIFT DINNER	1st SHIFT MEAL	DINING ROOM	BREAKFAST
Appetizers					
Soups					
Entrees					
Veg. & Potatoes					
Sandwiches					
Salads					
Desserts					
Special item					

Menu Administration

Administrative or management practices in any area of business make up the organizational structure that holds the plan together. Such practices in menu administration must accomplish the same thing—hold the menu together.

A menu should be a creative tool, not merely a mechanical contraption assembled without regard for the end result. A menu can be exciting or dull, depending on the enthusiasm of the person who plans it.

One of the management techniques that has been successful for many industrial foodservice operations is menu cycling. Cycling is a system of menu administration that plans a set of menus for 2 to 6 weeks and then repeats the "cycle."

In the average industrial foodservice, a 4-week cycle is the ideal length with four separate one-week menus being used. There are advantages to using 4-weeks as a cycle:

a) Only a limited number of repeats is needed for entree items and there is ample opportunity to change items for seasonal, cost or other reasons.

b) Menus can be controlled within the 4-week cycle of modern EDP accounting systems. Most major companies operate their accounting calendars on thirteen 4-week periods rather than the usual twelve calendar months.

c) Each week's cycle can be evaluated within the total of the four and the four evaluated as a group to assess achievement of check averages and food cost, as compared to the budget, on an accounting period basis.

While a 4-week cycle has advantages, in some cases it is either too long or too short.

EXAMPLES

In a school or college foodservice, students will sometimes complain about the repetition in a 4-week cycle as being too dull. Longer cycles can be used and, in some cases, menus can be planned for as long as a semester (15 weeks) at a time, incorporating holiday fare for special occasions, the training table for the athletes and other requirements into the menu cycles.

In hospitals, length of patient stay will vary with the type of hospital. A general hospital often has an average patient stay of 1-week. In such a situation, where your "guest" changes weekly, the menus can be the same each week. This does not include the employee cafeteria where the same people eat all the time and a longer cycle is necessary.

In a hospital heavily populated by old people, length of stay is considerably longer and longer cycles need to be used for patient menus.

Lengths of cycles vary depending on location and type of facility, but the principles and methods used to administer the menus via cycling stay the same.

Use of a menu idea book is another tool to be used in menu management. A menu idea book is nothing more than a 3-ring binder with index separator tab/pages to keep menu ideas by category. While there are many reference manuals and recipe books that can and should be used for ideas, consolidating the ideas you get from them into a single "idea" book suited to your needs can be a great tool.

Begin your menu idea book by cataloging the items on your first four cycles of menus and adding ideas as these menus are changed. You will find that within a short time you will refer to your own idea book more and more and outside references less and less. However, be careful not to become too inbred, using only the ideas catalogued in your own book; instead keep adding new items as you see them. There are many sources of menu ideas. Every time you eat in a restaurant, every time you are invited out to dinner, new menu ideas are passing your way. Industry magazines offer many menu ideas in articles and in advertisements. Gather them all and put them in your menu idea book and then use them.

Who should perform these administrative functions and also do the menu planning?

In a small location operated by a chef/manager, he does everything involved in managing the unit and this includes preparing the menu. In the larger location, an imaginative person with knowledge of food can be selected. This may be yourself as the manager, the chef, the production manager if you have one, the cafeteria supervisor or a committee made up of all of them. In many cases your client (or the plant trade union) retains authority to approve the final menu. Where this situation exists, make every effort to get the person or group who must approve the menu to take part in the original planning. This will save you much unnecessary criticism and time spent reworking your menus.

As an administrative tool, use a menu planning form. Fig. 40, p. 126, shows one form for planning menus for the various types of industrial foodservices. This type of form allows administrative control over the function of menu planning, offers an easy method of filing, and facilitates review for new planning. You can design a form of your own, get a set of forms from the average food wholesaler or distributor or be provided one by your employer if you work for one of the industrial caterers. No matter where it originates, such a form should be available and be used on a continuing basis.

Administrative aids to menu planning include maintaining a good reference library of cookbooks, recipe manuals, magazine articles and other similar materials. If you purchase one book a month, dovetailed with your other purchasing effort, you will soon have a helpful reference library on hand to assist in menu administration and planning.

Numerous organizations regularly prepare menus suitable to various needs, particularly in the health care field. The American Hospital Assn. has a variety of publications and diet manuals; the National Restaurant Association and various State Associations all publish references that are valuable aids to menu planning. Industry publications are another very useful source of reference.

Action—Menu Management

The A for Action in menu management is the key control factor in achieving the desired end result—a happy customer within controlled costs. Since happiness is relative, having a happy customer and keeping a customer happy are two different things but, by and large, your efforts as a manager toward managing your menu should include the following three weekly activities:

1) Review sales daily—summarized weekly for "units" of sale of each major menu item (i.e. entrees, large salads, specials, etc.). Compare their sale this time with previous times and determine whether popularity is holding or declining. Take action to correct items that are declining. A chart can be helpful in this effort.

2) Review daily the summarized weekly check averages for each meal period breakdown by budget category. If you are projecting a 65¢ lunch check average, be sure each

Fig. 40—MENU PLANNING FORM

WEEKLY MENU MAKER For _____ Period _____

									Reminders

BREAKFAST
FRUITS
CEREALS
Other Foods
BREADS
BEVERAGES

NOON
First Course
MAIN DISH
VEGETABLE
SALAD
BREAD
DESSERT
BEVERAGE

EVENING
First Course
MAIN DISH
VEGETABLE
SALAD
BREAD
DESSERT
BEVERAGE

OTHER

PREPARED BY _____
DATE _____

APPROVED BY _____
DATE _____

menu cycle produces a 65¢ or better lunch check average. The weekly operating report is the tool used to report check averages and these should be religiously reviewed every week. When a menu cycle is changed, pay immediate attention to its effect on the check average as compared to the last time it was reported before the change took place.

3) Review weekly food costs by categories. If cycle one produces a 50% food cost, what was the breakdown of that cost by categories:

a) Meat, Fish and Poultry	_____%
b) Produce	_____%
c) Dairy	_____%
d) Baked Goods	_____%
e) Coffee, Tea	_____%
f) Groceries	_____%

Here again, the weekly report provides this informaiton. Any variances in cost in any category should be traced immediately to the menu to see if variations in menus caused variations in cost.

These three items—units of sale, check averages and food cost—should be compared weekly to the menu and its variations by the manager as part of his management responsibility. This comparison is the minimum management effort that should be expended on menus. In a hospital or school, these yardsticks are irrelevant but other similar evaluations must be made.

All three areas, menu planning, administration and management, are the portion of overall planning that affects every other area of the food operation. Menu variety affects production and service needs. Menu acceptance affects customers' attitude. Menu selection coupled with selling prices affects the food cost structure of the budget. Menus are, in effect, the heart of the foodservice operation and should, therefore, be given the highest priority among the many items brought to the manager's attention to assure their proper planning, administration and management.

XII: Coffee Cart Service

The great American "coffee break" plays an important role in the industrial foodservice operation. Almost every location, whether it be in business and industry, school or hospital, now recognizes the tradition of the coffee break.

Many years ago, employees worked long hours with only one meal break at mid-shift. With the coming of the industrial revolution, manufacturers soon learned that factory employees were more productive at the dull repetitious work of assembly line jobs if short work interruptions were taken every few hours; because of this discovery, the "coffee break" was born. Today, plant employees often have one or two break periods written into their union/management work agreements and the majority of American workers are given either one or two break periods during the work day. For the industrial foodservice operator, this means serving one or two additional meals, even though they are only light snacks, usually only a beverage and "something" with it. Providing coffee break service is accomplished in various ways. As we shall see in this review, however, the guide to making it happen is still the basic:

1) OBJECTIVE

2) P-O-A—meet the objective

The objective may be a smaller portion of the overall unit objective but, nonetheless, it is still an objective and it can only be achieved by proper planning, organization and action.

Establishing the Objective

The answer to the question who will be served what, where and when establishes the objective. For example:

1) In a plant with 4,000 employees on 3 shifts, the employees may be provided with a coffee wagon at their work station midway between the start of their work shift and the mid-shift meal period. The service may be repeated again midway between their meal period and the end of the shift—or—they may be allowed a 10-minute break twice a shift as scheduled and have vending machines available nearby.

2) In an office building with 2,000 administrative employees, there may be one morning and one afternoon coffee cart service at their work area location, supplied by a coffee cart working out of the employee cafeteria.

In either instance, where a cart is used, it means bringing the foodservice to the employees rather than having the employees go to the foodservice. Different companies have individual policies on when the service is scheduled and what routes and stops the cart will make, but all coffee cart services have common problems and can be managed in the same general way.

Planning the Service

The first step in planning the cart service is to assess the total number of carts needed. Usually one cart will serve a population of 200 people. This can vary if distances to be travelled are too great in a plant or if elevator service causes major difficulties in a high rise building, but basically a population of 200 can be serviced from each cart.

Planning the Menu

The second step in planning the cart service is to establish the menu. The coffee cart menu will vary depending on the kind of shift services available in the manufacturing plant, the time of day the coffee run is provided and the personal tastes of the customers. There are two basic categories for all coffee cart menus:

1) Beverages
2) Something to "go with" beverages

Let's break them down separately.

Beverages consist primarily of hot coffee, sometimes hot tea and an assortment of cold beverages. Coffee is usually dispensed black, but sometimes it is also dispensed with milk or cream already in it. Where coffee with milk/cream is served, it is usual to have two thermos urns, one dispensing black coffee and one with milk/cream.

Hot tea is usually dispensed as hot water from a thermos urn with the tea bag added separately. Occasionally, hot chocolate powder, soup concentrate, bouillon, Sanka, Postum, and other items that utilize hot water are offered where a specialized need exists, however, these are the exceptions rather than the rule. Cold beverages usually consist of fruit juices on morning shift runs, especially orange juice and various other pre-portioned cold drinks such as milk, canned soda, containers of iced tea, orange and grape drink and similar items. Again in special situations the special preferences of a particular work force are recognized and items are added that satisfy them. In some instances, the cafeteria may "package" a favorite drink of a particular group and offer it on the coffee wagon.

Sales mix of the various beverages will vary with the time of day and the geographic locale. In the office building, coffee is the main beverage sale on the morning run although in some manufacturing plants in warm climates, a cold beverage may be a heavy sales item on the same run.

"Something With It"

The "something with it" portion of the cart menu is as varied as areas, people and circumstances. Primarily, the offerings break down as follows:

Morning Service—The morning service, for a first shift in a manufacturing plant or the first service in an office building, is usually a variety of donuts, pastries, hard rolls and what would normally be classified as breakfast rolls and/or pastries. While the cart service is officially described as a "coffee break," it is often used as breakfast by many workers, particularly those in urban high rise office buildings.

Afternoon Service—The afternoon service of a first shift in a manufacturing plant or service for an office building will sell fewer items with coffee or other beverage. These will be cookies, brownies and other mini-dessert type pastries rather than the breakfast type pastry. A higher ratio of cold drinks to hot drinks is sold as compared to the morning service and the side items offered must be compatible. Fresh fruit is frequently offered and, in some cases, ice cream is made available.

Second Shift Service—Where a manufacturing plant operates coffee carts on a second and/or third shift, they generally repeat the same morning and afternoon service used on the first shift. Beverage sales are usually of the same sales mix as offered on the first shift but the other items offered must be compatible with the time of day and personal taste preferences of the employees using the service.

In general, the coffee cart menu should be kept as simple as possible and offer as few items as possible. The fewer items offered, the easier the entire operation is to provide for, administer and control. "Cycling" of pastry menus instead of offering the same "full line" of pastries every day is one of the many ways available to keep the service requirements to a minimum.

Planning the Cart

The coffee cart represents a portable cafeteria, one that is used for a portion of the cafeteria menu. The simplest form of coffee cart is a plain utility wagon with a coffee thermos and a tray of pastries. This type is used successfully in many areas. Where an existing unit is in operation and present equipment has already been provided, it must be used. Where a new cart is being ordered, some thought should be given to its design in relation to the performance expected from it. Finding a cart that will perform as wanted is preferable to just taking a "stock" model and then trying to adapt it to suit your needs. Many manufacturers' catalogs show pictures of "stock" carts indicating they keep them available in inventory. In most instances, these models were originally manufactured for a customer as a special order and then became standard stock items. When you inherit a cart, use it of necessity; when you are purchasing a new cart, design it to suit your specific needs.

Planning the Route Structure

Before planning the coffee cart route structure, an assessment of priorities is required. When making such an assessment, items to be considered include:

1) Scheduled hour of the mid-shift meal (lunch, dinner, etc.)
2) Starting and quitting times of the shift
3) Distances to be travelled from the point where carts are assembled to points of sale
4) Obstructions to a smooth schedule, such as the elevator in an office building
5) Union rules governing the break period in a plant or factory

All of these factors must be considered when planning the route of the coffee cart and there are often other difficulties. Wherever and whenever your cart starts its service, some members of the work force will complain that "The cart is too early for me" and wherever the route ends, some members of the work force will complain that "The cart comes too near lunch time."

When planning the route structure, it is wise to obtain the cooperation and help of the department in the company responsible for the employee foodservice. Getting someone from that level of management to participate in coffee route planning can eliminate unnecessary complaints. Where a strong plant union exists, the shop steward should participate in the "route decision." However, it is impossible to please all the employees of a facility with the timing of the route to their location and, therefore, getting the customer to participate in the route structure, via a labor/management representative, is of the utmost importance.

When detailing the structure of the cart route, there are some specific points that should be noted:

1) A route should not run over 1½ hours. While a population of 200 can normally be served in this time, if distance precludes this, fewer people should be served.

2) Routes should be scheduled so the cart goes to various "stops" that have been established at designated points for certain periods of time rather than to have the operator of the cart "stroll" and sell merchandise upon demand.

"Strolling" provides very slow service whereas "stops" provide fast service. The work force will become used to having the coffee cart at a particular location at a particular time and will accommodate themselves accordingly.

3) Routes should be published. All employees should know where the coffee cart stops and returns. Some employees are not always at the same work station every day at the same time.

4) And again, get management's participation and approval of route structure. At best, coffee carts are a difficult service to operate and incur many complaints about time, products available, etc., most of which are unfair. Making management establish clear-cut policy on who will be served, what—where—and when is of primary importance to coffee cart route structure.

Administrative Methods of Organized Control

Just as the main cafeteria uses a production system to control production, the coffee cart service must have controls. The cart service also has a need to control its cash handling to assure that the proceeds from all retail sales find their way back to the cafeteria.

Various methods exist to accomplish this task. However, the most effective is the use of the daily control card, Fig. 41, p. 132. This device allows the manager to insert the amount of merchandise issued, returned and sold and to calculate the value of sales, twice daily, for the same route and operation. From the sales information garnered from a study of daily sales, the manager can evaluate the requirements of each cart and each area for beverages and other items.

Predicting Unit Sales

A coffee cart will sell a particular number of "units" (i.e. cups of coffee, pieces of pastry, containers of milk) in a rather well-defined pattern. While it is necessary to have sufficient merchandise on each cart for each service to assure that there are few run-outs before the end of the service, it is also desirable not to be over-stocked thus having many leftovers that may have to be disposed of as waste.

This can be accomplished by predicting anticipated sales and stocking the wagon in accordance with your prediction. This should be a manager's or supervisor's decision and should not be left up to the service worker. A daily summary sheet showing actual sales for each cart, of each item, for each run is necessary for this purpose. Fig. 42, p. 133, shows the sheet

Fig. 41–DAILY CONTROL CARD, COFFEE CART SERVICE
SERVICE CORP.   COFFEE CART CONTROL

Cart No:					Date:						
A.M. ITEM	ISSUE	RET'D.	SOLD	@	AMOUNT	P.M.ITEM	ISSUE	RET'D.	SOLD	@	AMOUNT
PASTRY				.15		PASTRY				.15	
ROLLS				.15		CUP CAKES				.10	
MUFFINS				.10		DONUTS				.10	
DONUTS				.10		COOKIES				.10	
BAGELS				.15		PRETZELS				.10	
BIALYS				.15							
COFFEE				.15		COFFEE				.15	
MILK				.15		MILK				.15	
TEA				.15		TEA				.15	
OR. JUICE				.15		OR. JUICE				.15	
SANKA				.15		SANKA				.15	
						SODA, B'd				.15	
						SODA				.15	
	TOTAL SOLD						TOTAL SOLD				
	TOTAL RECEIVED						TOTAL RECEIVED				
	OVER OR (SHORT)						OVER OR (SHORT)				

used by an office building location with 36 carts in service twice daily. Upon analyzing the information on this form you will find that units of sale, total sales and sales mix will vary from day to day, but as often as not will repeat themselves on the same day each week. Monday will match Monday, Thursday will match Thursday, etc., but Monday and Thursday may not match.

In a heavily populated office building, the population has patterns and trends that will show up in coffee cart units and dollars of sales on a daily basis. These must be considered when making your sales predictions to stock your coffee carts. The information from the daily control card, as summarized on the weekly form, supplies the necessary information to allow you to make an intelligent decision on sales predictions.

Controlling Cash on the Cart

Controlling cash from sales of a coffee cart is not as simple as taking cash register readings and evaluating the resulting sales. The average coffee cart attendant is provided a small cash bank and then leaves the cafeteria premises to be on his own, unobserved by manage-

Fig. 42–DAILY COFFEE CART RECAPITULATION

USAGE RECAPITULATION OF UNITS SOLD.   DATE: DAY:

Cart No.	Pastry	Cup Cake	Donut	Cookie	Pretzel	Coffee	Milk	Tea	Orange	Sanka	Soda	Soups			
0															
1															
2															
3															
4															
5															
6															
7															
8															
9															
10															
11															
12															
13															
14															
15															
16															
17															
18															
19															
20															
21															
22															
23															
24															
25															
26															
27															
28															
29															
30															
31															
32															
33															
34															
35															
36															

ment, to provide retail sales. Here, again, various methods exist to control the cash collected in cart service, but the control card method is the most effective.

The Retail System

In order to use the control card effectively, each cart is issued merchandise which is entered on the control card as "units" of inventory by selling price. Example: All 15¢ cakes and pastries are inventoried as "15¢ items." All 25¢ products are inventoried as "25¢ items." This is called the "retail system" of inventory. In effect a "dollar" of cash or a "dollar" in retail value of merchandise is still a "dollar." The cart attendant is to be held responsible for the "retail" value of her merchandise in the same manner as she is held responsible for the cash value of the coins and bills supplied as part of her change fund.

Bulk beverages, such as coffee, are difficult to count as "units" so these are converted to "cups" (by issuing and controlling the number of paper cups provided the attendant) as units of value on a retail basis. Another method of controlling bulk beverage usage is by measuring the beginning and ending inventory of a thermos urn, using a graduated "dip stick." This is simply a clean wooden stick with graduations of half-gallon measurements evaluated as markings cut into the wood.

One very successful method of controlling cash on a cart service is to "sell" the inventory to the attendant and require return merchandise or cash at the end of the run. This is the method used by stadium operators at baseball and football games. There are some labor agreements where this is not possible; in that case the retail system should be used.

As mentioned, there are many systems, but as a successful manager you *must* use a system. It is a grave mistake to delegate the planning and cash control of a coffee cart to the same worker who operates the cart.

In summary, establish the objective of the cart service in relation to service need and financial limitation; then evolve P-O-A to accomplish your objective. A well operated cart service requires a *complete* management effort if it is to be succesful.

XIII: Sanitation and Maintenance Management

Sanitation and maintenance management are two of the most neglected areas of management in the average industrial foodservice. All too often these two spheres of operation are *allowed to happen* rather than being *made to happen*. As the manager of an office building or plant foodservice or school or hospital foodservice, you are responsible for the health of the employees, students or patients you serve insofar as the food they consume on your premises is concerned.

The U.S. Dept. of Public Health lists 62 diseases that are communicable from man to man. Forty percent of these can be transmitted by food or food-borne bacteria. If you will reflect on that statistic for a few minutes, you will readily see the importance of sanitation and maintenance in your foodservice and the phrase "Sanitation Management" may take on a new and more important meaning to you.

The phrase "Sanitation Management" is used here and extended to "Sanitation and Maintenance Management," to apply the word *Management* in these areas as it has been previously applied to other aspects of industrial foodservice operations. It is also true in this instance that (1) a manager must make things happen to achieve a specific objective and (2) an objective can be achieved by:

P—plan
O—organize
A—act

P-O-A can be applied to sanitation and Maintenance Management, as well as to any other facet of the business.

First, let's define the objectives of a good Sanitation and Maintenance Management Program:

1) To keep the foodservice premises and equipment in an acceptable condition to maintain and meet required health standards.

2) To provide food (meals) for employees/students/patients to meet those same health standards.

3) To keep foodservice employees of the unit sufficiently knowledgeable about health standards and disease hazards so they can achieve the results outlined in objectives 1 and 2.

Sanitation and maintenance planning go hand in hand as part of a total plan to maintain an acceptable operation; keeping foodservice equipment in the proper state of operation and repair helps to keep the sanitation program up to par.

EXAMPLE

1)   A malfunctioning dish machine will not properly sanitize utensils.

2)   Insufficient hot water will not wash soiled ware clean.

3)   Improperly working thermostats will not control food storage temperatures in holding boxes or refrigerators.

There are numerous other examples that can be cited, but these three should make the point.

An industrial foodservice manager has many special problems in the area of sanitation and maintenance that are not present in a commercial restaurant operation. Among them:

1)   Coffee cart operations; food prepared on one shift and served on another; remote patient service by non-food personnel; student labor and many other factors all present problems of food handling, sanitation and employee training that are unique to industrial foodservice. These require special knowledge and skills not required of the average restaurant manager.

2)   Since the equipment in the average industrial operation is usually owned by the company/school/hospital that is being provided the service, it must be maintained by them and it is often difficult for an industrial foodservice manager to obtain his fair share of budget money or maintenance department time and effort to fill his operating needs.

A good manager must plan a course of action to achieve his objectives despite obstacles and a good industrial foodservice manager must realistically assess his problems and plan a course of action to assure proper Sanitation and Maintenance Management.

The Plan

Remembering the five M's—let's begin with *men*. A specific person must be made responsible for basic sanitation and maintenance. If you are a chef/manager, this responsibility is now added to all your other duties, since you are in charge of everything anyway.

If your unit is slightly larger, it is often possible to designate one of your utility men as a "head man" to enforce your program and achieve your goals in area cleaning and maintenance and the chef or a supervisor is then used to take over the sanitation training of employees and various other aspects of the program. In any event, one or more *specific* supervisory personnel must be made *specifically* responsible for part or all of your program. Those assigned must be provided with the materials and knowledge to carry out their responsibility and there will then be ample assistance available to you. This is described in *money, materials, methods* and *machines* as a further part of the plan.

Sufficient *money* must have been made available, via proper budgeting, to have sufficient *men* and *materials* available to perform all the required work properly. Later, in this chapter, cleaning schedules will be drawn up for the specific job to show you how to assess needed labor and materials. The point to be made here is that man/hours means *money*. A budget that provides the needed money must be achieved.

Cleaning materials go beyond the mop and broom today, as modern chemicals, detergents, soaps and other cleaning agents have made clean-up a lot easier. There are various competent national companies that sell cleaning supplies. Many companies manufacture products that wash dishes, pots, cut grease, sanitize work surfaces, clean floors and can be used in other routine work. Select a qualified company to provide the cleaning materials you will need; then investigate their products and become completely familiar with their use. Many of these companies provide booklets or printed pages that show and/or tell how their cleaning materials should be used on equipment. In selecting your supplier, make sure he has good explanatory material of this type and make it available to employees assigned to do the cleaning.

Hold to a minimum the number of cleaning products selected to do the work in your unit, introducing as many multi-purpose cleaners as possible. At the same time, don't skimp on the use of special items for special purposes. Sanitizing work surfaces, deliming coffee urns and dish tanks, cleaning garbage cans and disposal units, all require special treatment. In choosing cleaning materials, deal with a company that has a reliable product line; prepare a list of the materials you plan to utilize and provide your *men* with these materials and they will accomplish your goals.

Proper cleaning *methods* are essential if you are to obtain the most for your *men, money and materials.* There are many ways to wash a pot, mop a floor or sanitize a piece of equipment, but the proper method will save money by utilizing the least number of man/hours and the smallest amount of cleaning materials. Here again a cleaning supplies company can be of assistance to you together with the various local agencies, food suppliers, food equipment companies and other similar sources. There is a method recommended for cleaning each piece of equipment in your unit. This literature is usually part of the original shipment, coming with the equipment, or can be secured by writing the manufacturer or calling their local representative. Every reliable company that sells foodservice equipment wants it to wear well and, as a result, give them a good reputation.

Foodservice equipment will only give good service if it is properly cleaned and maintained. Company representatives are readily available to provide this information and it takes only a letter or phone call to bring them to your operation. Many food purveyors also provide instructional material detailing the way to handle the equipment that prepares their products. Coffee companies and frying oil purveyors, in particular, do an excellent job of providing "methods" of using and cleaning coffee equipment and/or deep fat fryers in order to enhance the use of their product. Other companies provide material on the correct use and care of slicers, steamers, etc., all of which can and should be part of your *methods* for sanitation and maintenance planning.

The national cleaning supply companies are a comprehensive source of help. Many of them prepare detailed booklets on how to use their products successfully; booklets are available that outline methods for cleaning almost anything. Either the whole manual or portions of it can be incorporated into your plan for achieving proper sanitation methods.

The *machines* portion of your plan consists of such items of equipment as the scrubbers, portable steam cleaning units and similar pieces of equipment. Properly selected machinery can also be an aid in reducing the man/hours required to accomplish a job. The portion of your plan that comes under the heading of maintenance and assures that all equipment is in proper working order will be discussed later. Very often a manager will either work without the proper equipment or with equipment that is not functioning properly; this only complicates his operating problems.

Good *machines* are most important to good sanitation standards and must be part of the plan to achieve them. Some equipment, such as a portable steam cleaner, that is used less frequently cannot always be provided for in a current budget. In such a case, renting that equipment on a periodic basis, or sub-contracting out work such as steam cleaning on a periodic basis, can get the job done. Meanwhile, continue to request capital funds every year in your budget for your own equipment. One of the best ways to "force out" some capital money is to spend, for rented or sub-contracted equipment, an amount annually that is equal to or in excess of the cost of the equipment. Know what machines you need to do your job, then find a way to provide them for your people.

The Organization

How can you go about organizing your plan with its men, money, materials, methods and machines to accomplish the job? First of all, remember that organization puts structure into your plan and holds the plan together.

Every location should have a complete set of cleaning schedules that cover every area and every piece of equipment on the premises. Every manager should also have a continuing program of indoctrination in basic food handling and sanitation techniques for new employees with reminders for older employees. This may sound formidable, but it is not. Let us start out with the preparation of a cleaning schedule or manual for your operation.

Step One

Prepare an 8½ by 11 in. form on a stencil or ditto machine, as shown below:

CLEANING SCHEDULE		
UNIT _____		AREA _____
OR PIECE OF EQUIPMENT: _____		
WHAT to clean	*HOW to clean it*	*WHEN to clean it and WHO will clean it*

Step Two

Designate every area of your operation or piece of equipment as follows:

EXAMPLE–*AREA*
  Area 1–Cafeteria Entrance
  Area 2–Dining Room
  Area 3–Scullery
  Area 4–Cafeteria Service Area
  Etc.

EXAMPLE–*EQUIPMENT*
  Coffee Urn
  Deep Fat Fryer
  Dish Machine
  Etc.

Step Three

Using a separate form for each area, stand in the middle of that area and look around. Check everything you see that must be cleaned. Start with the floor, walls and ceiling–go on to the furniture and equipment that is in the area and make a complete check list of everything you see.

Step Four

Now prepare your cleaning schedule by asking yourself the questions:

1)   *What* is to be cleaned?
2)   *How* is to be cleaned?
3)   *When and by Whom* will it be cleaned?

The rest is simply a matter of doing a thorough job of seeing and writing and this only has to be done once. Fig. 43 and Fig. 44, pp. 140-141 are examples of such schedules that were actually prepared at two operating units–one a plant and one an office building. As for setting up equipment cleaning standards, forms and assistance, as mentioned previously, can be obtained from a cleaning supplies company. An example of the kind of cleaning instructions that are suggested are the following instructions from one booklet that tells how to clean a griddle.

DAILY

1.   Scrape all loose soil from the surfaces as soon as equipment is cool enough to work with.

2.   Wet the surface with water. Sprinkle liberally with _____. Brush
     (insert product name)
     with a good, nylon bristled brush. Clean the edges and sides of the griddle.

3.   Scrape off the loosened soil and rinse with a wet sponge.

4.   Empty and wash the scrapings pan and replace it.

5.   As griddle starts to heat again, brush with food grade vegetable oil. Keep the base of the griddle, the top and sides of the stand, the back plate and the spatter shield thoroughly clean at all times to avoid odors, off-flavors and infestation.

With proper forethought and effort you can easily *organize* a cleaning manual that specifically suits your own unit. Combine this manual with your man/hours planning to schedule the required help to accomplish the job.

Fig. 43—CLEANING SCHEDULE

UNIT:_____   AREA: KITCHEN

WHAT To Clean	HOW To Clean	WHEN To Clean WHO To Do Job
1. WALK-IN REEFER	Remove merchandise from shelf. Wash shelves with ammonia solution. Straighten merchandise. Mop floor with soap and water.	After lunch meal 3 P.M.; BY kitchen man with chef responsible.
2. ICE MACHINE	Empty cube and shaved ice from bins. Wash interior with detergent solution. Rinse down with clear water. Wipe bottom dry. *Be sure to rinse all soap away.*	Once weekly on Saturday; BY beverage man.
3. 60 GALLON URN	Fill with three (3) gallons water. Wash with urn brush. Use gage brush in glass tube. Drain. Dismantle faucet. Wash with _____ and water. (insert product name) Rinse. Reassemble.	Three times daily after each time used: BY beverage man.
3. 60 GALLON URN	*Fill* with fifty (50) gallons warm water. Add 8 oz. baking soda. *Boil* solution for ten minutes. *Drain* and rinse until clean. Dismantle faucet and soak in hot _____ solution. (insert product name) Rinse and re-assemble.	Once weekly on Saturday; BY beverage man.
4. FREEZER	1. Wipe exterior with ammonia solution. 2. Remove all food. Wipe interior with ammonia solution.	Once daily; BY kitchen man (3 P.M.) Once weekly on Saturday. BY kitchen man.
5. PASS-THRU REEFER	Wipe out interior and exterior with clean cloth soaked in ammonia solution. Remove empty trays, consolidate foodstuffs.	Twice daily; 2:30 P.M. BY kitchen man; 8:30 BY night cook.
6. COOK'S WORK TABLES	Wash with hot water and detergent. _____ Wipe down (insert product name) with clean cloth and ammonia or _____ solution. (insert product name)	After every use; BY Chef/Cook or kitchen man.

Fig. 44–CLEANING SCHEDULE II B, CAFETERIA FOODSERVICE AREA

AREA	HOW	WHEN AND WHO
1. Stainless steel counter tops and fronts	Wiped off with soap and water solution and polished. Spots and stains removed as they appear.	Daily in the A.M. by the cafeteria porter.
2. Tile wall behind counter	Washed with soap and water solution.	Daily by food runner.
3. Menu Boards	Lint and dust removed by using damp cloth.	Weekly by cafeteria servers and checkers.
4. Coffee storage space	Shelves emptied and wiped off with soap and water solution.	Daily by coffee server.
5. Door behind counter	Wiped off with soap and water solution.	Weekly by dish runner.
6. Self Leveling Dish Dispensers	Cleaned outside and in with soap and water solution.	Weekly by utility workers.
7. Ice Cream cabinets and lids	a. Scrape from cabinet and wash with ammonia and water solution. Allow to dry and wipe clean.	Weekly by counter girls.
Lids	b. Wipe off with soap and water solution.	Daily by person working station.
8. Ice Cream Dipper well	Drained and washed out with soap and water solution.	Daily by person working ice cream station.
9. Milk dispenser and storage area	Wiped off with soap and water solution.	Daily by person working ice cream station.
10. Pie cabinets and work table tops	Cleaned daily with soap and water solution. Table tops wiped off after each use.	Cafeteria servers each day.
11. Storage refrigerator behind counter	a. Cleaned with soap and water solution.	Daily by cafeteria worker.
	b. Cleaned with ammonia and water solution.	Weekly by cafeteria worker.
12. Cold display shelves for salads, pies and desserts	a. Defrosted and washed with soap and water solution.	Daily by cafeteria servers.
	b. Disassembled and cleaned with ammonia and water solution.	Four times a year by utility men under supervision of the manager.

Scheduling the cleaning man/hours is a little more complicated than planning foodservice man hours and must take local conditions into consideration. However, there are some standards that can be established by an operation for such tasks as area cleaning and other large scale projects. These standards can be established by placing a crew, or an individual, on the job under proper supervision, then having the job done and timing the man/hours needed to accomplish it.

Various "methods manuals" can be purchased that indicate how many man/hours are required to clean specific square foot areas of floor tile, carpeted floor, ceilings, etc., similar to a time study basis. Local cleaning "contractors" can be called in who use various "tables" to "bid" a job in their business and have established standards for required man/hours. All of these sources can be used to organize your plan into effective action.

One of the better tools of organization for cleaning and sanitation in a large operation is the use of an opening and closing check list. The pilot on every airplane flight, for take-off and landing, is required to use a check list so the pilot can make sure he has accomplished every routine task by actually checking it off. The safety of his own life, as well as that of his passengers, depends on how completely and thoroughly he does the routine tasks necessary at take off or when landing the plane.

The health and safety of your patrons and yourself (you eat there too) can depend on equal attention on your part to completing, or having a supervisor complete, a simple opening and/or closing check list. Fig. 45, pp. 143-147, is a closing check list that is actually in use at a large New York office building location that provides foodservice for 3,000 employees, in part of two floors of a 50-story building.

Another check list of value is a sanitation check list; it should be used to make regular routine health inspections of your own premises. Most localities have health inspectors visit the premises periodically and some localities require that you maintain a self-inspection system. One company in New York City uses the self-inspection system form, Fig. 46, pp. 148-149. This company has its managers inspect their own premises once a month using the "self-inspection report." The completed report is then kept on file, with notations of the actions taken on all deficiencies, for the local Board of Health inspector to see when he comes in. It is a most effective system and makes a manager see himself as others (e.g. the Board of Health) see him.

Check lists really work and are worthy of attention as part of your sanitation and maintenance *organization* effort.

Before setting up the *ACT* portion of P-O-A to achieve our objective, the management of maintenance must be considered.

Maintenance in an industrial foodservice situation can sometimes be difficult to accomplish. When your equipment is owned by the "plant" and the plant maintenance supervisor doesn't like the foodservice "people," you have a problem. It is not at all unusual to find that the maintenance people of the plant, hospital or school feel that foodservice equipment should *not* break down or that foodservice people are negligent with their equipment. Therefore, they will not provide the needed service. There are as many ways as there are people to encourage cooperation from the maintenance department and using your own ingenuity coupled with the occasional free cup of coffee or lunch can be the answer. There are also

Fig. 45–SANITATION CHECK LIST

2ND FLOOR	2ND FLOOR
Dining Area	
Tables _____	Under Counter Units _____
Chairs _____	Ice Cream and Milk _____
Condiment Stands _____	Beverage Section _____
Water Coolers _____	All self-leveling dispensers _____
Flooring (Circulation Area) _____	Floors _____
Flooring (other) _____	Corners _____
Carpet (Service Area) _____	Open Drains _____
Waitress Stations _____	Top of Reach-in Box _____
Planter Boxes _____	Stainless Panelling & Doors _____
2nd Floor Office _____	Ceramic Walls _____
Cashiers Station _____	Tray Slide Area _____
Self Service Beverage (Bay 1) _____	**Service Area–Bay II (hot)**
Wall Mounted Ash Trays _____	Ice Machine Area _____
Service Area–Bay I (cold)	Tray & Silver Area _____
Ice Machine Area _____	Dumbwaiters _____
Tray and Silver Area _____	Sinks _____
Dumbwaiters _____	Mobile Carts _____
Sinks _____	Hot Food Section _____
Mobile Carts _____	Under Counter Warmers _____
Sandwich Section _____	Salad & Dessert Section _____
Salad and Dessert Section _____	Ice Cream & Milk _____

(cont.)

Fig. 45—SANITATION CHECK LIST (cont.)

2ND FLOOR		2ND FLOOR	
Service Area—Bay II (hot)		Hot Food Equipment	————
Beverage Section	————	Salad & Dessert Area	————
All Self-leveling Dispensers	————	Sub-Veyor Section	————
Floors	————	Floors	————
Corners	————	Corners	————
Open Drains	————	Open Drains	————
Top of Reach-In Box	————	Top of Reach-In Box	————
Stainless Paneling	————	Stainless Doors	————
Ceramic Walls	————	Ceramic Walls	————
Tray Slides Area	————	Hoods	————
Service Pantry		Mobile Equipment	————
Ice Machine Area	————	**Supervisor's Office**	
Beverage Pick-up Area	————	**Soiled Dish Room**	
Waitress Tray Station	————	Carts	————
Ice Cream Area	————	Sink	————
"Compressor Area"	————	Floors	————
Dumbwaiters	————	Walls	————
Sinks	————	Corners	————
Steam Table Area	————	Drains	————
All Self-leveling Dispensers	————	Sub-Veyor Flights	————
Sandwich Prep	————	Sub-Veyor Shelving (around bet's)	————
Stainless Shelving	————	Floor of Subveyor Room	————

3RD FLOOR		3RD FLOOR	
Men's Room		Shelving	_____
Locker Area	_____	Mobile Carts & Dollies	_____
Toilet Area	_____	Conveyor Belts	_____
		Soiled Dish Tables	_____
Women's Room		Sinks	_____
Locker Area	_____	Walls	_____
Toilet Area	_____	Floors	_____
		Corners & Molding	_____
Vinyl Floor Corridor		Clean Tray Racks	_____
		Clean Silver Section	_____
Kitchen - General		Exhaust Hoods	_____
Freight Lobby	_____	**Coffee Cart Area**	
Receiving	_____	Carts	_____
Corridor to storeroom	_____	Vacuum Containers	_____
Corridor to Time Clock	_____	Sterilizing Section	_____
Floors	_____	Floors	_____
Corners and Molding	_____	Walls	_____
Walls	_____	Corners	_____
Dumbwaiters	_____	Coffee Urn	_____
Janitors Closets	_____		
Walk-In boxes (outside)	_____	**Bakery**	
Dish Room Area		Floors & Drains	_____
Machine	_____	Walls	_____

(cont.)

Fig. 45–Sanitation Check List (cont.)

3RD FLOOR		3RD FLOOR	
Bakery (continued)		Floor Drains	————
Sinks	————	Hoods	————
Reach-In Box (top)	————	Mixer	————
Proof Box	————	Utensil Rack	————
Electric Range Area	————	Work Tables	————
Do-Nut Area	————	Mobile Carts	————
Work Tables	————	Steamer	————
Roll Divider	————	Chef's Refrigerator (top)	————
Stove	————		
Tilt Kettle	————	**Pot Wash Area**	
Baker's Store Room	————	Machine	————
Wall Cabinet	————	Drain Boards	————
Mobile Racks	————	Sinks	————
Mixers	————	Hood	————
Utensil Rack	————	Clean Pot Table	————
Mobile Bins	————	Pot Racks	————
		Floors	————
Cooking Area		Walls	————
Ranges	————	Drains	————
Fryers	————	Corners	————
Broilers	————		
Roast Ovens	————		
Kettle Table	————	**Meat Prep**	
Steam Kettles	————	Fish Box (top and sides)	————

3RD FLOOR		3RD FLOOR	
Meat Prep (continued)		Mobile Racks	_____
Sinks	_____	Floors	_____
Equipment	_____	Walls	_____
Work Tables	_____	Corners	_____
Butcher Block	_____	Sinks	_____
Floors	_____		
Walls	_____	**Garbage Room**	
Drains	_____	Walls	_____
Corners	_____	Floors	_____
Hot Food Carts	_____	Garbage Cans	_____
Salad Prep		**Storeroom**	
Work Tables	_____	Shelving	_____
Cabinets (tops)	_____	Floors	_____
Shelving	_____	Walls	_____
Equipment	_____	Corners	_____

some good administrative practices you can follow that will assist effectively; here are a few to be considered:

1) Prepare a card file, listing each piece of equipment that appears on your cleaning schedule, plus all motors, compressors and other equipment that services your operation, on a separate 3 x 5 file card.

2) Obtain the maintenance schedule for the oiling, greasing, fan belt changing and similar activities required for each piece of equipment and list it on the file card.

3) Prepare a request for maintenance on a specific scheduled basis for each piece of equipment that requires scheduled maintenance and give it to the responsible person for this area. Keep a schedule posted on each card showing maintenance that has actually been performed.

These three simple steps will provide you with the administrative controls you need as well as creating a cooperative atmosphere between you and the maintenance group since this program demonstrates that you have as high a regard for equipment as they do. Your record will also show where excessive breakdowns have occurred because your own people have not taken the proper care of their equipment and such a record will help you to pinpoint necessary training needs.

In some cases, outside service contracts are used to maintain equipment; this is primarily the practice with refrigeration, heating and air-conditioning equipment. Sometimes small equipment, like cash registers, are more readily maintained by a service contract. Office building operations are more likely to use an outside contracted service than a manufacturing plant where competent maintenance personnel already exist. Assess your own individual case and plan maintenance in the same way that you have planned your sanitation program and as an intregral part of it.

The POA FOR SANITATION AND MAINTENANCE

Now to *ACT*—and bring the package together. The initial and continued training and supervision of your personnel is necessary in all areas of foodservice but of particular importance in this area. Much of the training that must be accomplished requires outside assistance. In some areas, all food handlers must, by law, attend classes provided free by the local department of health or other governmental agencies. Various training films, audio-visual programs and other materials are available from purveyors of detergents, coffee, meat and other supplies. Such aids are also available from the U. S. Dept. of Health, Education and Welfare, the U. S. Dept. of Agriculture, other government agencies and from various trade associations and industry publications.

In areas where workers do not speak English well, but do speak Spanish, these training materials are often available in Spanish. Various operating directions for dishmachines are available in Spanish and can be posted at appropriate locations for the non-English speaking machine operator. The U. S. Dept. of Health, Education and Welfare's publication, "Sanitary Foodservice," is an instructor's guide to providing a full course in sanitation for the foodservice worker; it contains much good material.

Training—plus supervision—plus personal effort to make your plan succeed by using your organized administrative tools are the key ingredients.

As I have stated before:

OBJECTIVE—PLUS—P-O-A TO MEET IT

can make it possible to accomplish both the sanitation and the maintenance management goals of your job.

Fig. 46–SANITATION INSPECTION REPORT

ADDRESS_____ TYPE OF ESTAB. _____ NAME_____ DATE

IN ACCORDANCE WITH SECTION 81.39 OF THE HEALTH CODE OF CITY OF NEW YORK
1. *Inspections of these premises must be made at not less than monthly intervals by a qualified person.*
2. *The findings of these inspections shall be kept on file on the premises for a period of 12 months.*
3. *These inspection reports shall be open to inspection by representatives of the Department of Health at all times.*
4. *Objectionable conditions found shall be immediately corrected.*

(X) IN BRACKET INDICATES ITEMS NOT COMPLIED WITH

A. OPERATION AND MAINTENANCE
 1. Perishable foods kept refrigerated prior to serving at 50°F or less ( ).
 2. Hot meats, gravies, etc. at steam table maintained at 140°F or more ( ).
 3. Custard filling chilled rapidly after preparation ( ); custard filled pastry properly refrigerated ( ).
 4. Hollandaise sauce freshly prepared and kept for maximum period of 2 hours ( ).
 5. Pork and pork products thoroughly cooked until there is no trace of pink color to prevent trichinosis ( ).
 6. Milk dispensed in single service containers or from approved dispenser ( ); within 54 hours age limit ( ).
 7. Milk and cream cans and bottles rinsed when emptied ( ); not reused ( ).
 8. Shellfish received from approved sources ( ); tags filed for 60 days ( ).
 9. Food stocks rotated regularly to avoid spoilage and assure freshness ( ).
 10. Prohibited insecticides and rodenticides used ( ).
 11. Silver polishes containing cyanide prohibited ( ).
 12. Premises free of rodent infestation ( ).
 13. Premises free of insect infestation ( ).
 14. No live animals kept on premises ( ).
 15. Ice cream dippers or scoops kept in clear, running water ( ).
 16. Dry sweeping of floors prohibited ( ).
 17. Metal slicers, grinders fruit juicers, cream urns, ice cream dippers pumps and fillers taken apart, washed and cleaned daily ( ); surfaces free of corrosion, pitting, or dents ( ).
 18. Bins, shelvings, containers, etc. cleaned before refilling ( ).
 19. Kitchen knives, forks, ladles, beaters, etc. clean and free of corrosion ( ).
 20. Unwrapped foods (cakes, pies, breadstuffs, etc.) protected from dust, flies, handling, etc. ( ).
 21. Foods properly protected from hazardous chemicals and cleaning agents ( ); exposed light bulbs ( ); loose wires, nails, screws, etc. ( ); insecticides, fumigants, rodenti-cides ( ); drip from overhead lines ( ).
 22. Stoves, griddles, broilers, fryers, etc. clean of grease and soot ( ); properly hooded and vented to the outer air ( ).
 23. Fans, hoods and ducts clean ( ); and in good repair ( ).
 24. Steam tables clean ( ); and in good repair ( ); proper temperature maintained ( ).
 25. Space between fixtures or counters, behind slicers, tables or shelving or under fixtures and cutting boards clean and free of food particles or scraps ( ).
 26. Dumbwaiter and dumbwaiter pits clean ( ); and in good repair ( ).
 27. Unused equipment kept clean or removed ( ).
 28. Planned daily cleaning program used ( ).
 29. Sanitation maintenance schedule posted ( ).
 30. Brooms, mops, brushes, pails, soap and detergents, etc. available ( ); and properly stored ( ).

B. WASHING AND STERILIZING FACILITIES
 1. Equipment adequate to 1) Pre-scrape and prerinse, 2) wash, 3) rinse, 4) sterilize all eating and drinking utensils after each use ( ); or single service used.
 2. Adequate supply of running hot water at peak periods ( ).
 3. Facilities for maintaining sterilizing water at 170°F ( ).
 4. Sufficient number of properly constructed baskets provided and permit utensils to be properly placed ( ).
 5. Adequate supply of glasses, silverware, cups and plates for peak periods ( ); suitable holders for paper cups provided ( ).

C. DISHWASHING MACHINE
 1. Clean and free of corrosion ( ); in good repair ( ); thermometers on wash and final rinse lines ( ).
 2. All surfaces of utensils adequately sprayed under pressure ( ); spray jets free from clogging ( ).
 3. Time of washing and sterilizing adequate ( ).
 4. Utensils properly racked ( ); not overloaded ( ).
 5. Wash water changed frequently ( ). Detergent added frequently ( ); automatic feeder working properly ( ).
 6. Scrap strainers cleaned frequently ( ).

D. WASHING AND STERILIZING OPERATION
 1. All utensils washed and sterilized after each use ( ); visibly clean to sight and touch ( ).
 2. Scraped, pre-flushed, washed in clean hot water (110°–120°F, by hand; 130°–140°F, by machine) with detergent, rinsed in clean water ( ).
 3. Sterilized at 170°F or higher, or approved chemical used ( ). Set aside to drain dry to avoid towelling ( ).
 4. Stored on clean shelves protected from rodents, insects, dust, splash, etc. ( ).
 5. Chipped or cracked utensils discarded ( ).

E. PERSONAL HABITS OF FOOD HANDLERS
 1. Clean hands and fingernails ( ). Hands washed frequently, *especially after using toilet ( ).*
 2. Clean, washable outer garments ( ); also caps or hair nets ( ).
 3. Spitting prohibited ( ); smoking prohibited where food is prepared ( ).
 4. Hands kept away from nose, mouth, pimples, hair, etc. ( ).
 5. Moistening fingers with lips to pick up paper napkins or wrappers prohibited ( ).
 6. Street clothing in clean closet or locker ( ).
 7. Soiled linens, aprons, coats, etc. kept in closed container ( ).
 8. Food handled unnecessarily ( ); appropriate utensil supplied ( ).
 9. "Wash Hands" Sign ( ).
 10. Completed acceptable course in food handling ( ).

F. ALL EQUIPMENT
 1. Sanitary construction readily taken apart and easy to clean (no open seams, dead ends, rough or pitted surfaces. ( ).

(Cont.)

Fig. 46–SANITATION INSPECTION REPORT (cont.)

F.   ALL EQUIPMENT (Continued)
2. Tops of work tables and cutting boards smooth ( ); free of cracks and crevices ( ).
3. Equipment in good repair ( ); no rust, corrosion or defects ( ).
4. Refrigerator temperatures below 50°F ( ); accurate thermometers provided ( ).
5. Water supplied equipment and iceboxes properly drained ( ).
6. Area around equipment accessible for cleaning ( ).

G.   WALLS, FLOORS, CEILINGS (throughout premises)
1. Ceilings and Walls: Clean ( ); free from holes, cracks, crevices ( ); scaling ( ); holes around pipes, cables, etc. ( ).
2. Floors: Clean and dry ( ); free from holes, cracks and crevices ( ); holes around pipes, cables, etc. ( ); eroded to obstruct the pitch to drain ( ); floor drains, if any, clean and in good working order ( ).

H.   LIGHTING AND VENTILATION
1. Lighting fixtures in good repair ( ); adequate ( ); bulbs, and globes clean ( ); glass in fixtures over exposed foods protected from breakage ( ).
2. Skylights clean ( ); in good repair ( ); protected against rodent invasion ( ).
3. Fans clean ( ); in good repair ( ).

I.   TOILET COMPARTMENTS
1. Properly lighted ( ); window in good repair ( ); duct, if any, unobstructed ( ), fan, if any, in good working order ( ).
2. Clean seats ( ), clean bowls ( ), clean urinals ( ); bowls tight at base ( ); all plumbing in good repair ( ); doors self closing ( ).
3. Handwash basins clean ( ); running hot and cold water ( ); Soap ( ); individual towels ( ); toilet tissue ( ).
4. "Wash hands before leaving toilet" Sign ( ).

J.   LOCKER ROOMS
1. Properly lighted and ventilated ( ); clean ( ).
2. Lockers clean ( ); in good repair ( ); rat proof ( ); nothing stored on top or underneath ( ).

3. Number adequate ( ); completely separated from food storage ( ), and preparation room ( ).

K.   FOOD STORAGE ROOMS
1. No rodent infestation ( ); no insect infestation ( ); stored materials neatly arranged ( ).
2. Floor racks or platforms removable ( ); at least 12 inches from floor ( ).
3. No drips from overhead lines onto foods ( ).
4. Bins, shelves, and containers clean ( ).

L.   FOOD STOCK
1. Foods stored off the floor ( ).
2. Loose and unwrapped foods stored in rodent proof and insect proof containers ( ).
3. Food free from spoilage or contamination by rodents ( ) insects ( ).
4. Foods inspected at least weekly ( ); perishable foods refrigerated ( ), inspected daily ( ).
5. Unwholesome foods immediately separated, *denatured*, marked "Condemned," and removed promptly ( ).

M.   GARBAGE RECEPTACLES
1. Garbage in metal receptacles with tight cover ( ); emptied and cleaned daily ( ).
2. Adequate number ( ); not leaking or broken ( ); stored away from foods ( ).
3. Garbage station clean, rat proof, free from flies and odors

N.   CELLAR
1. Free from rubbish, ashes, and useless material ( ).
2. Stored material neatly arranged ( ); away from walls and off the floor ( ).
3. Gratings, louvres, windows, doors, and other openings to the outer air ratproof ( ).
4. Covers of sewer traps and clean out pits tight and in place

O.   REAR YARD
1. Clean, free from debris, loose garbage, stagnant water, etc. ( ).
2. No preparation and storage of foods in any rear yard, alleyway, public hall, etc. ( ).

ADDITIONAL RECOMMENDATIONS OR REMARKS

_____
_____
_____
_____
_____
_____
_____

XIV: Foodservice Vending

Foodservice vending is an integral part of the employee foodservice and is rapidly becoming a dominant force in industrial foodservices. Almost every new industrial foodservice has some form of vending related to it. Many of the older foodservices are adding vending to their facilities or changing a portion of their facilities to vended foodservice.

In order for today's foodservice manager to succeed, he must know:

    a. The economics of foodservice vending.
    b. The management structure of the vending branch operation.
    c. The basic principles of vending machine operation.

Although it is not necessary for the unit manager to be a vending machine mechanic, he must know as much about the operation of food vending machines as he does about the other foodservice equipment in his unit. He must also know the problems inherent in selling food through vending machines, in order to intelligently plan and direct his management effort to achieve his own overall objectives.

Vending History

Vending is not a new phenomenon; it actually dates back to 215 B.C. A Greek, named Hero, wrote in a book of that time, entitled "Pneumatika," about a machine that dispensed holy water when "five drachmas" were inserted. Very little is known of the ultimate disposition of Hero's original work, but an Italian translation in 1587 of Hero's book contained an illustration of his machine. Amazingly enough, the design of the holy water dispenser described in 215 B. C. closely parallels the design of a modern cream dispenser of today. The drawing on the next page is similar to the one that appeared in the Italian translation in 1587.

The next time vending appeared was about 1675 when it was used in English taverns. A type of snuff and tobacco box, with a locked lid that was released by the drop of a coin, was utilized to sell these products to tavern patrons and was the forerunner of cigarette vending. Some of these tobacco boxes were brought to America in the early Colonial days and still exist in the hands of private collectors.

In 1822, an Englishman named Richard Carlile built a book vending machine, designed

Holy Water Coin Operated Dispenser
Circa 215 B. C.

to outwit local laws of censorship and release him from responsibility for selling blasphemous material. The machine worked but it did not absolve him from legal prosecution for selling this type of material.

Some 35 years later, in 1857, an Englishman named Simeon Dunham was issued what appears to be the first patent for an automatic selling device. This was a postage stamp vender. This patent lay dormant for another 30 years before the automatic sale of stamps began to take hold.

As patents began to protect the inventors of new machinery, the inventors of vending equipment began to protect themselves with world patents under the international patent laws.

In the United States, the first financially successful vending venture was that of Thomas Adams who, in 1888, founded the Adams Gum Co. Adams had machines designed to sell his products on the "el" platforms of New York City. He later formed the American Chicle Company which still thrives today. Automatic merchandising of gum products on transit system platforms is still an important part of their business.

Through the years, vending moved through various product lines from postage stamps to perfume, even to divorce papers. In Corinne, Utah, at one time, divorce papers could be obtained by inserting $2.50 in silver dollars or half dollars into a machine. Further processing by local lawyers and courts was required, however, in order for the divorce to become effective.

Automatic food merchandising and selling was first successfully undertaken by the Horn and Hardart Automats around 1902. This was the forerunner of the use of foodservice vending in modern industrial cafeterias. The real catalyst, however, was the invention of the fresh brew coffee machine in the early 1950's. This completely revolutionized the by then already large vending industry and brought that industry and the foodservice industry together. Large vending companies began to acquire foodservice companies, first on a regional basis, then on a national basis. Thus, today's giant national industrial food and vending service corporations were born.

Vending Today in Industrial Foodservice

In today's manufacturing plant, vending is used extensively to provide hot and cold beverage service to the plant worker and, to an increasing degree, hot and cold foods as well.

The National Automatic Merchandising Association, located in Chicago, keeps current figures on national sales volume of various types of vended merchandise. Their 1970 report shows that $6.223 billion of foodservice vending is now done annually, mostly in industrial foodservice operations

The industrial food vending operation today usually consists of a bank of machines dispensing hot beverages (primarily coffee), cold beverages, hot foods, cold foods, milk and ice cream. Candy and cigarette machines are also added and are highly profitable, but these are not considered part of foodservice vending. The foodservice manager of a modern industrial foodservice installation may provide a manual cafeteria at a "main" installation and vended operations at satellite locations or on second and third shifts. Vended foodservice is particularly applicable where the total population is small, the area remote or the off-shift population too small to support a manual cafeteria.

The Economics of Vending

Many industrial foodservice operations are fully subsidized by the profits made available from vending machines that sell items to the company's employees. The food vending catering companies are highly skilled at using vending profits to offset cafeteria losses and, in so doing, can operate on a combined profit and loss basis without direct subsidy from the client. Where does all the profit come from and how is it achieved? Let's look into the basic economics of vending and find out.

A modern coffee machine brews each cup of coffee *after* the consumer has inserted a coin to make the purchase. After the coin is inserted, the machine then brews a single cup of coffee, adds liquid sugar and/or powdered non-dairy cream product, as may be desired by the consumer, and the sales transaction is completed. Approx. every 200 sales transactions, a service man arrives and re-stocks and services the machine; this requires less than one-half hour of his time. If it takes two days for the machine to sell 200 cups of coffee, the routeman will need to service that machine only once every two days.

Compare that method of selling with one where a cafeteria worker makes fresh coffee every half hour in a manually operated cafeteria, sells it to a customer, takes the cash in payment and must clean up after he has made the sale. It is easily seen that "manual" selling can be profitable only when sufficient sales volume exists to support a worker, while "vended" selling without need for a full-time worker can make a profit on a smaller volume of business daily.

Vending profits are generated by machines that store merchandise that requires little or no attention and will remain in salable condition until the consumer wishes to make a purchase. Hot beverage and cold beverage machines fit into this category.

Prepared food vending does not fall into this category and does not usually generate a profit. A hot or cold food vending machine requires the same or more attention to its product as is required by food sold manually. These machines must be stocked with food at frequent intervals and leftovers must be removed and fresh food inserted. The leftovers are frequently disposed of as a total loss.

Pastry, milk and ice cream machines, which are termed food machines, do make a small profit since these items have a known period of shelf life and require minimum attention from the routeman. The routeman's time can be planned within a reasonable schedule, similar to that set up for coffee and soda machines.

The basic economics of vending are that the highest volume of the sales mix is in items that generate high profit and the minor volume of the sales mix is in products which make little or no profit. The resulting sales mix usually allows a good margin of profit. A recent study shows the following national averages of total sales through vending machines in industrial operations:

Cigarettes	30%
Candy	12%
Cold Beverages	13%
Hot Beverages	25%
Ice Cream	3%
Milk	3%
Hot and Cold Food	14%

You will note that 14 percent of the sales mix is in unprofitable hot and cold food and 86 percent is in profitable merchandise. These are national averages and do not hold true at single locations.

There are installations in which the sales mix does not generate the desired profit, but they are the exceptions rather than the rule and are usually subsidized.

Projecting Vending Sales and Costs

Just as an industrial foodservice must project an annual budget, a vended foodservice must project its potential sales and costs *before* an investment is made in equipment. The capital investment to equip the industrial foodservice operation is usually provided by the company requiring the foodservice, but the investment needed to equip a vending operation is almost always provided by the company providing the vending service. In order to assure a fair return on its investment, the vending company usually has its branch manager prepare a "pro forma" to project sales and costs, evaluating the potential net profit. The pro forma is the same as a budget. Unless the projected net profit provides a reasonable return on investment, the vendor will not make the installation.

Projecting Sales

The usual system used to project potential vending sales is to project on a "per capita" per week basis, by product line.

"Per capita sales" means sales potential averaged on a per-person-of-population basis per week. Sometimes this is expressed in "units," as with cups of coffee and sometimes it is expressed in dollars, as for cold food. In either case, it is converted into dollars per person per week and projected annually by product line and then summarized for all products in total.

EXAMPLE

A manufacturing plant with 3000 day-shift employees has a cafeteria serving breakfast and lunch but it also provides coffee break and satellite location vending plus cigarette and candy vending. The price structure in the machines is:

Coffee	15¢
Cold drinks	15¢
Pastry	15¢–20¢–25¢
Candy	10¢–15¢
Cigarettes	50¢

Potential sales for this operation would be projected in the following manner:

Item	Per Capita Units	Selling Price		Per Capita Dollars
Coffee	_____x	15¢	=	$ _____
Soda	_____x	15¢	=	$ _____
Pastry	_____x	20¢ av.	=	$ _____
Candy	_____x	12½¢ av.	=	$ _____
Cigarettes	_____x	50¢	=	$ _____
			Total Estimated Weekly Sales	$ _____

By entering the number of cups of coffee, cups of soda, pieces of pastry, pieces of candy and packs of cigarettes that you can expect to sell per person per week, the total weekly sales can be easily projected.

All the major industrial foodservice companies have an experience factor to rely on to assist them in assessing per capita sales of each product line. These factors will vary greatly by area of industry, type of worker population, area of the country and ratio of male to female employees. A steel mill in a cold upstate New York area may project five cups of coffee and two cups of cold soda per person per week but the same industry in a hot southern state could project the opposite sales mix.

A New York City location in an office building could project one piece of pastry for every three cups of coffee sold but a Midwestern city would project less than half that ratio.

Nevertheless, information does exist that can be evaluated to project sales in a rather precise manner and this makes vended foodservice sales easier to estimate than manual food service sales.

Projecting Product Costs

The foodservice operator uses the phrase "food cost" to indicate the percentage of food cost to sales. The vended foodservice operator uses the phrase "product cost" to indicate the percentage of food and other product cost to sales. This is a commonly-used business term in foodservice vending.

The foodservice operator has a major task in evaluating the unit cost of every item he sells during the course of a week, but the vended foodservice operator does not have that problem. All his machines, except hot and cold food, sell items under a stable cost structure. This allows him to project his product cost, by product line and in total, with relative ease. Let's take the above example and project it one step further to assess product cost of the potential sales. The following table can be used to make an assessment of product cost:

Item	No. of units sold		Average cost per unit		Total Cost
Coffee	_____	X	_____	=	$ _____
Soda	_____	X	_____	=	$ _____
Pastry	_____	X	_____	=	$ _____
Candy	_____	X	_____	=	$ _____
Cigarettes	_____	X	_____	=	$ _____
Other	_____	X	_____	=	$ _____
			Total Product Cost		$ _____

An alternate method of projecting both sales and product cost uses a percentage of sales by product-line system and can be shown on a form designed to show annual sales and merchandise cost as in Fig. 47, facing page.

Projecting Gross Profit

Gross profit is a common business term used to indicate the difference between sales and product cost. This *gross* profit becomes the amount of money available for all of the usual business expenses over and above product cost.

EXAMPLE

If sales are $100,000 annually and product cost is 40%, gross profit is $60,000.

Sales	$100,000	100%
Product Cost	-40,000	40%
Gross Profit	$ 60,000	60%

All other operating costs must be paid from *gross* profit and sufficient *net* profit must be left to warrant the initial capital investment and to make the business venture worthwhile. Completing a form similar to Fig. 47, facing page, permits the operator to have all the necessary information to assess his gross profit.

Other Operating Costs

Since all other operating costs must be paid for from the gross profit, a projection of what these costs are and how much they will be must be made. There is very little difference between manual and vended operations in this section of the pro forma or in methods used to project these costs for the industrial foodservice operation, although some different and additional categories do exist. Let's look at these individually and discuss them further.

Labor Costs

An industrial foodservice would never have less than one employee, but a single bank of machines serviced by a routeman would not normally require a full-time employee. In a case such as this, a percentage of the routeman's time would be allocated as labor cost.

In a large plant where a number of machines were in service, one or more routemen would be permanently assigned as "resident" routemen and their full wages would be allocated as labor costs. When this situation occurs, the cost of supervising these routemen is often allocated as "supervisors" in "Branch Expenses." (See Fig. 48, p. 158 for organization

Fig. 47–VENDING PRO FORMA SALES AND MERCHANDISE COST

Sales Product/ Type	Vending Price	Per. Cap. Weekly Sales	Annual Gross Sales	% Merch. Lost	Amount Merch. Cost
Coffee	15¢	$_____	$_____	_____%	$_____
Cold Drink	15¢	$_____	$_____	_____%	$_____
Canned Soda	25¢	$_____	$_____	_____%	$_____
Cigarettes	60¢	$_____	$_____	_____%	$_____
Candy	10-15¢	$_____	$_____	_____%	$_____
Pastry	15-25¢	$_____	$_____	_____%	$_____
Milk	15¢	$_____	$_____	_____%	$_____
Ice Cream	20¢	$_____	$_____	_____%	$_____
Hot Cans	35-50¢	$_____	$_____	_____%	$_____
Food Merch.	35-60¢	$_____	$_____	_____%	$_____
Total All Products		$_____	$_____	_____%	$_____

structure of branch). In either case, a labor projection is made, using a format similar to the following:

LABOR AND RELATED COST PROJECTION

Type	No.	Hrs. per Day	Regular Weekly Cost	O/T or Premium Cost	Annual Cost 52 Weeks
Serviceman	____	_____	$_____	$_____	$_____
Hostess	____	_____	$_____	$_____	$_____
Mechanic	____	_____	$_____	$_____	$_____
Supervisor	____	_____	$_____	$_____	$_____
Delivery	____	_____	$_____	$_____	$_____
Other	____	_____	$_____	$_____	$_____
				Total	$_____
			Cost related to payroll–% of	Total	$_____
			Total Annual Labor and Related Costs		$_____

Decisions on what types of workers will be assigned and how many man/hours they will work are the only decisions required to complete the labor cost projection. Wage rate, cost of overtime premiums and payroll related costs are usually readily available.

Direct and Indirect Operating Expenses

Some additional direct and indirect operating expenses are attributable to the unit installation and these must be assessed. These can be listed as follows:

DIRECT EXPENSES		*INDIRECT EXPENSES*	
Vehicle Expense	Commissions (Salesmen)	Rent	Guard Costs
Installation Costs	Other	Utilities	Others
Retail Sales Tax	Repairs	Telephone	
Licenses and Permits			

Fig. 48–ORGANIZATIONAL STRUCTURE OF VENDING BRANCH

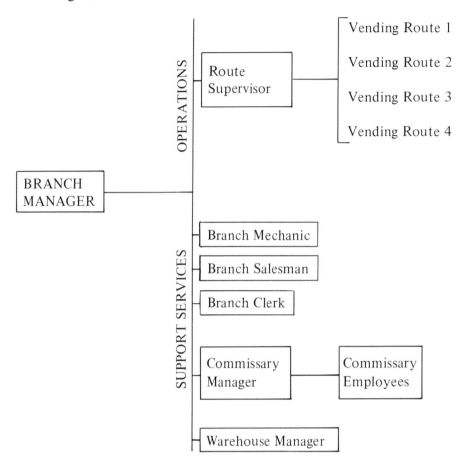

Notice that indirect expenses include items, such as rent and utilities, not normally found in an industrial foodservice budget but often found in a vending pro forma.

Depreciation

A major item in the vending pro forma is depreciation. Vending machines are almost always supplied by the vending company and these machines represent a major part of the capital investment of their business. As with all capital investment, it is depreciated; that is, the investment cost is written off over a number of years. This dollar amount of depreciated write-off must be included in the pro forma.

The depreciation period differs on various machines and from company to company but, by and large, the following format is used to evaluate annual depreciation:

Product Type	No. of Machines	Unit Cost	Total Cost
Coffee	_____	$_____	$_____
Soda	_____	$_____	$_____
Candy	_____	$_____	$_____
Cigarettes	_____	$_____	$_____
Pastry	_____	$_____	$_____
Milk	_____	$_____	$_____
Ice Cream	_____	$_____	$_____
Food Merchandise	_____	$_____	$_____
Hot Canned Food	_____	$_____	$_____
Other	_____	$_____	$_____

Total Cost $_____

Divided by ___ Years, Depreciation equals $_____

In addition to vending machines, various other equipment is often used with them that requires a different schedule of depreciation and this other equipment is usually evaluated separately but on the same kind of table. It may include:

Microwave Ovens
Condiment Stands
Coin Counting Equipment
Delivery Vehicles
Other

The Pro Forma

Summarizing the sales and costs is done on a form called the "job pro forma." This is the same as preparing a budget for an industrial foodservice.

VENDING PRO FORMA

Annual Sales Projection	$ _____	100%
Estimated Product Cost (subtract)	$ _____	___%
Gross Profit	$ _____	___%

Other Costs

Labor and Related Costs	$ _____	___%
Direct Operating Costs	$ _____	___%
Indirect Operating Costs	$ _____	___%
Annual Depreciation	$ _____	___%
Total Other Costs	$ _____	___%
Net Job Available for Commissions and Profit	$ _____	___%

Vending Commissions

You will notice the statement that the *net* available figure is available for *Commissions and Profit.* Commissions are an important part of the vending business, since a "bid" is usually made by the vending salesman to obtain each vending location. It is often necessary to bid a high commission and the ability to assess how much commission one can afford to pay is extremely important.

The vending industry operates on a "return on investment" basis. This means the profit must equal a satisfactory return on the capital investment made. In addition, a satisfactory percentage of profit on sales must be achieved. This percentage varies from company to company. In all instances, the simple arithmetical procedure of subtracting the necessary profit required from the potential profit available provides the answer to the question, "How much commission can be bid?"

EXAMPLE

Sales	$100,000	100%
Available for Commissions and Profits	$ 30,000	30%
Capital Investment	$ 40,000	
Return on Investment Desired*	$ 18,000	

The difference between the "available" and the "desired return" can be bid in commission.

EXAMPLE

Available		$30,000
Return	Subtract	18,000
		$12,000 potential bid for commissions

This does not necessarily mean that $12,000 *will* be bid on commissions, but only indicates the *maximum* amount that can be bid. The area of commissions is complex and commissions require an extensive study of their own. For this example, it is necessary only to show the student of industrial foodservice management how a vending pro forma is prepared and how vending commissions are determined.

In summary, the economics of vending are almost always profitable, easily predictable via a pro forma and a major economic force in industrial foodservice. The successful industrial foodservice manager must be aware of how and where these profits come from.

Management of the Vending Branch

In the major corporations involved in industrial foodservice and vending, the primary level of organization responsible for operating the vending route is the Vending Branch. As the manager of an industrial foodservice operated by a professional company, you would have the vending portion of your service handled by the nearest branch. If you are employed as the manager of a company-operated foodservice which also utilizes vending, you might well sub-contract that service to a similar branch. In either instance, you should have a knowledge of how a branch operates in order to obtain the maximum service that is available.

Each vending branch handles customers within a specific geographic radius of its location, usually up to 50 miles. Distance will depend entirely on the area, road accessibility, traffic conditions, etc. A vending branch in the center of a large metropolitan city may only cover a 5-mile radius and a branch in a suburban area where traffic is light and the roads good may cover up to 50 miles. Time, rather than distance, is the controlling factor and a branch

---

*Example only—not a specific figure.

tries to operate within a "one-hour" radius of its center of operation.

Fig. 48, p. 158, shows the organizational structure of an average vending branch. Note that it is broken down into Operations and Support Services.

Operations for a branch are run by a route supervisor who directs and controls the efforts of the various routemen. The route supervision is supported by the services of a vending mechanic who performs necessary repairs at locations and operates a small repair shop at the branch and a vending commissary manager who prepares and packages the necessary food for the hot and cold food machines. The commissary is nothing more than a kitchen similar to an industrial foodservice kitchen; however, its products are not sold over the cafeteria counter but are packaged for the routeman's use.

The branch clerk performs the administrative chores necessary to maintain an accountability system and the branch salesman looks for and sells new business. The warehouse manager maintains an inventory of all the necessary supplies to keep the branch operating.

A large branch may have special counting rooms to handle the large amounts of coins that must be counted; a large branch may also have many route supervisors, salesmen or clerks. The size of the branch merely extends the number of people in each job category but does not change the organizational structure of the branch. By understanding how a vending branch operates, the industrial foodservice manager can provide the most effective service. If you are a location manager with an extensive vending operation on your premises, you should visit the branch that provides that service and become familiar with its operation and its people.

Principles of Machine Operation

In the average industrial facility, a customer who is not satisfied with the service he receives from a vending machine will complain to the food operating people who are available. Often the foodservice manager is responsible for the servicing of some of the hot and cold food vending machines that service second and third shifts in remote areas of operation. In some cases, the vending route man working as a "resident" route man reports directly to the foodservice manager. In any case, the industrial foodservice manager needs a working knowledge of how vending machines operate in order to be able to supervise a worker intelligently or relate his operation to the services of a branch operation. Numerous publications and manuals exist which will provide detailed mechanical explanations and these should be studied. This book will only attempt to provide a basic orientation to machine operation.

Coin Mechanisms

All vending machines have one thing in common—coin mechanisms. Every machine accepts coins in some combination and, as often as not, will give the customer change if it is appropriate. The coin mechanism is the source of most mechanical problems and most consumer complaints, as well as the source for most abuse by the customer.

These are complicated mechanical devices of various designs but in most modern machines they are easily removed and replaced. The only knowledge required by the route man is how to remove a faulty mechanism and replace it with one in working condition. The faulty one is returned to the shop, repaired and made ready for another installation. If you are mechanically minded, you may learn to repair a coin mechanism, although it is not necessary. If you can operate a cash register, take its readings and change its tapes, you can learn to replace a coin mechanism with ease.

Food Machines

The machines you are most likely to be required to know how to make adjustments on are the hot and cold food machines. The cold food machine is nothing more than a large refrigerator with a mechanical lazy susan in it. Usually windows and/or doors are unlocked by a solenoid release when the correct number of coins is inserted. The operator must learn how to open the large front door, load each compartment with a different food item, close the door and lock it. No other mechanical knowledge is required.

What is required is some common sense and some knowledge about the food products being inserted. The average vending route man treats these foods as "product;" the foodservice worker regards them as "foods" and treats them accordingly. Inspection for quality, rotating of stock, removing of stales are all necessary for the successful operation of this piece of equipment. More product complaints are received from the cold food machine than any other machine. As the foodservice manager of the operation you will receive these complaints; therefore, you should take an active interest in that machine's operation.

Hot food machines are of two types: the mechanical can vendor and the larger display machine that dispenses hot casseroles. As often as not, "hot" casseroles are stored cold in the cold food machines and the customers heat the food themselves, using an adjacent microwave oven on a self-service basis. Hot food display machines are being used less and less, but are similar to the cold food machine, the only difference being that the "box" is heated and not refrigerated. Hot foods deteriorate rapidly and this type of machine must be serviced often.

Hot canned food machines are identical to cold canned soda machines. All the cans of food are kept hot all the time and care must be taken that the machine is not overloaded as this will cause deterioration of its contents. The same problems of rotating and eliminating spoils exist as with the cold food machines but this problem is compounded since the food cannot be seen through the can to allow inspection.

Beverage Machines

The two primary beverage machines most often used are coffee and soda machines. These are produced by many manufacturers and in many varieties. In the early days of vending, such companies as the Interstate Vending Company and Canteen Corp. manufactured their own machines in order to maintain a superior machine and so obtain a greater share of the operating market. This is no longer true and these companies have long since sold off their manufacturing divisions. There are now numerous companies manufacturing high quality hot and cold beverage machines but, here again, they have common characteristics which can be easily understood by the foodservice operator.

Coffee Machines

Some coffee machines dispense coffee only and some also dispense hot chocolate and consomme type soups. All beverage machines dispense a cup at a time and, therefore, have as a common design the cup turret and the mechanical devises necessary to "drop" the cup.

Coffee machines are of two basic types:

a) Single cup machines
b) Batch brew machines

Most machines now in use are single cup machines that actually brew one cup of coffee at the drop of the correct coin combination. Brewing takes place in the same manner as the food operator uses to make coffee. A small filter is placed over a small "mixing chamber" and the correct amount of coffee is "dropped" on top of the filter. A hot water release allows the correct amount of water to flow through the fresh coffee and on down to the cup. Dried powdered coffee lighteners, usually non-dairy, and dry or liquid sugar are "dropped" from separate tanks.

There are as many different engineering combinations as there are manufacturers of machines and it is not necessary for the foodservice manager to know how each type of machine operates. What is necessary for him to know is how to make coffee manually as in a cafeteria. Good coffee requires clean, fresh water, good quality products and clean equipment. This is probably even more important in a vending machine than in a manual operation.

Regardless of whose equipment services your employees, you should learn enough about the machine to know the location of the brewing chamber, water filter and product storage bins and to check them periodically to be sure the service man does as good a job on them as you expect your cafeteria worker to do on your coffee urn. Most vending route men never face their customers; therefore, they are not normally customer-oriented. If you should become responsible for coffee vending at your installations, take an active interest in the maintenance as well as the servicing of your coffee machines.

Cold Beverage Machines

Cold beverage (soda) machines do exactly what the soda equipment on your cafeteria lines does. They dispense pre-mix, post-mix or canned soda only at the drop of a coin. The larger machines dispense up to four varieties of post-mix products with or without flaked ice.

Internally, the machines have much in common with the coffee machine, particularly in that they have a coin mechanism and a cup dispenser and the same operating problems found in any machine. In addition, they have the same equipment you have in a manual operation. A post-mix machine has syrup tanks, a small carbonator, a small ice flaker machine, water supply and filters and the various controls required to dispense them all when a coin activates the machine.

A pre-mix machine has the same tank of pre-mixed product that is used in a cafeteria to replace the carbonator and syrup tanks. These are usually used where there is no available water hook-up. A canned soda vender is the same as a hot canned food machine but larger and refrigerated instead of heated. It requires only an electrical outlet and is used at locations where pre-mix is not desired.

Cold beverage machines require a proper mechanical service as does the carbonator, ice machine and water supply system required in your manual foodservice. If you are skilled in the maintenance of this equipment in your foodservice (which most managers are not), you can handle the smaller equipment behind the vending door. If you are like the average manager, you will require a service man and mechanic to handle it. However, when it comes to sanitation, you are as skilled as, or more skilled than, the service man.

Service men are prone to spill syrup and cause other sanitary problems similar to those caused by foodservice workers. However, servicemen are not as quick to do the proper cleaning job after creating this sanitation problem. Here again, as with the coffee machine, your own efforts to assure that the proper procedure is followed by the route man will give you a good serviceable machine and a happy customer.

Cigarette, Candy Machines

These are all mechanical machines with the more modern ones dispensing their products on a first-in, first-out basis that automatically rotates their stock. Mechanically, they are very simple with the coin mechanism being the only complication and it usually is easily replaceable. If you have learned enough to service a food or beverage machine, you can easily service a candy or cigarette machine.

It is not at all unusual now for a cafeteria operation to have a cigarette and/or candy machine operated by the foodservice manager with the servicing of the machine performed by the cafeteria workers. Companies that manufacture machines will sell them direct to you and find you a local mechanical service back-up.

Other Vending Equipment

Various other pieces of vending equipment exist and new equipment is marketed every day. Dollar bill and five dollar bill changers, heating ovens and numerous devices rise and fall in popularity depending on the service need and serviceability of the equipment. The increased use of vending machines to provide a foodservice for the industrial operation is an established fact. The industrial foodservice manager of tomorrow will have to be as knowledgeable about the economics and operation of foodservice vending as he is about the operation of the manual foodservice.

Much has been written about this topic and the National Automatic Merchandising Association maintains an excellent library and also prepares much of their own material on the subject. The numerous industry magazines keep operators up-to-date on trends and new equipment and an operator should subscribe to some of them. Vending machines in operation today could well be obsolete next year, but the economics and operating procedures governing their use are basic management methods that will continue to apply. The truly professional industrial foodservice and cafeteria manager will become an expert in foodservice vending management as well.

XV: Insurance and the Unit Manager

Every management man in every area of business needs some knowledge of insurance. The topic of insurance is extremely complex, having many variations, specialty areas and types of coverage but this need not deter the industrial foodservice manager from becoming sufficiently knowledgeable about insurance to meet his needs as a manager. This chapter is intended to acquaint the unit manager or student with the various areas of insurance and how they relate to him and his operation; it will not delve into the technicalities of the insurance field as they are too complex for this study. These are left for further independent study as may be required by each individual.

First, let's give a simple answer to the question, "What is insurance?" My own simple answer is "Financial coverage for a degree of risk." The higher the degree of risk, the higher the cost of the premium payment; the lower the degree of risk, the lower the cost of the premium payment. Good management keeps insurance costs as low as possible by lowering the "risk" to the insurance company and the chance that they will have to "pay out" on a "risk loss." The definitions of "risk," "payout" and "risk loss" are self-evident.

RISK—The odds against something happening that will cause the insurance carrier to be liable for a loss.

PAYOUT—The paying of money by the insurance carrier to the person or company that makes a claim.

RISK LOSS—The amount of money the carrier pays on the "payout."
These are not insurance company definitions, but my own terms used to translate "insurancese" into every day words we can all understand.

Types of Insurance

There are many types of insurance, covering a wide variety of potential risk. For our purposes in relation to industrial foodservice, I have defined insurance coverage as being of three types; policies which cover risk loss for:

1. People
2. Things (Property)
3. Money

People Insurance

The most common form of "people" insurance is the individual life insurance that many people carry. This has little bearing on the industrial foodservice operation. The people insurance you are likely to deal with in industrial foodservice will insure the people who come and go on your operating premises. These are your employees and your customers.

EXAMPLE

A customer who accidentally hurts himself on your premises or gets sick from eating food served in your unit has a valid insurance claim against your operation. An employee who gets hurt from an on-job accident has a valid claim against his employer.

In most states, an employee who has an accident or an illness off the job has a claim against his employer via state mandated disability insurance. These are all examples of "people" insurance. Other examples are hospitalization coverage, group life insurance and pension plans often provided by the employer. These are all insurance coverages on people. Let's review them one by one.

People Insurance—Public

Public and Product Liability—General Liability—This policy protects the unit operation against claims from the customer for personal or property damage caused by the operator. Typical coverage is for up to $300,000 of bodily injury to each person or up to $1 million for each accident. Coverage usually includes premises liability, operation liability and products liability. Other liabilities, often covered by the same policy, insure against fire, water damage and advertiser's liability. Sometimes insurance in excess of the $1 million coverage is purchased; this can go up to $5 million with coverage known as an Umbrella Policy. This is a low cost extension of the general liability policy.

Typical claims filed under this group of liability policies are:

1) A customer breaks a tooth on a foreign object found in the operation's food.
2) A customer has internal injuries from swallowing a small piece of metal that "curled off" from the can opener and found its way into the beef stew.
3) A customer slips and falls on a wet floor in the dining area and breaks a leg.
4) One of your employees injures a customer by spillage or by bumping him with a bus cart.
5) One of your operation's coffee carts causes damage on its route.
6) A major accident occurs in a plant due to negligence of one of your vending men during his rounds of servicing machines.
7) A hospital has an epidemic caused by bad food prepared by one of your employees.

There are many more examples, but these illustrate the types of coverage you receive from your general liability policy. Both the persons and the property of the patrons are covered.

People Insurance—Employee

Various state and federal laws mandate that an employer carry insurance to protect his employees for injury on the job and/or injury off the job. In addition, some employers provide their employees with additional coverage for life, medical and other risks.

Workmen's Compensation insurance is a mandatory coverage to protect the employee for medical costs and loss of income due to a job-related accident. The cost is borne 100% by the employer. The several states have different laws covering Workmen's Compensation but, in almost all cases, this coverage is placed by the employer with a private insurance company specializing in that type of insurance. The cost is based on the number of employees there are and the gross amount of their payroll with the premium usually based on a percentage of the payroll dollars.

A large number of claims in a single year will increase the premium cost and a small number, or no claims, in a given year will decrease the annual premium. Premium rates vary in each geographic locality, with the original rate usually established by the State Controller as a "book" rate. This book rate is paid for the first one to three years after which the operation's own "experience" rating takes over and the insurance premium will then be adjusted up or down, depending on the experience in the unit.

A "safe" house, free from claims, can lower insurance costs for Workmen's Compensation as much as 10% from the original book rate. Conversely, an excessive amount of claims can increase the cost 10%, making a 20% swing in the overall cost entirely possible.

The Federal government prepares a variety of documentary summaries about current Workmen's Compensation laws and rates for all 50 states. These can be obtained by writing to the Supt. of Documents in Washington, D. C. and requesting a current listing.

State disability insurance is mandatory in most states with the cost also borne 100% by the employer. As with Workmen's Compensation, the coverage is usually placed with a private carrier specializing in that type of insurance. Benefits usually provide up to 50% of weekly wages, with a maximum amount per week and with coverage usually up to 26 weeks. Coverage usually begins on the eighth day of the employee's absence. Variations will exist in different states.

Social Security Insurance (F.I.C.A.)—Social Security is basically retirement insurance provided by the Federal government and paid for equally by the employer and the employee. A percentage of each worker's wages on a certain base (5.3% of a base of $9,000 in 1972) is paid by each. Congress enacts laws periodically which change both the percentage and the base as well as the coverage. Recent changes brought Medicare, a hospitalization plan for those over 65, into being and also increased the insurance rates. Social Security is a specialized field of insurance with a large number of varying benefits and much information is available about it. This can be obtained at any Social Security field office.

Unemployment Insurance is another type of government-operated "people" insurance that is paid for 100% by the employer. The purpose of this insurance is to provide income for personnel leaving your employ and not obtaining other employment.

There are two types of unemployment insurance:
1. State Unemployment—Coverage for 26 weeks
2. Federal unemployment—Coverage after State Unemployment runs out for an additional 13 weeks.

Premiums are paid in the form of a payroll tax as low as under 2% of payroll and as much as over 4% of payroll, with a maximum base established as taxable payroll. This amount differs from state to state. The rate covering the Federal 13 weeks usually costs 20% of the rate for the State 26 weeks.

EXAMPLE

IF   26 weeks State Unemployment costs 4% of base payroll. . . .
13 weeks of additional Federal coverage will cost 20% x 4% or .8% of base payroll.

The total cost of unemployment insurance will vary depending on the rate of employee turnover in your unit. The more "ex" employees applying for and receiving unemployment insurance, the higher your costs will be. A good manager keeps happy employees. One of the fringe benefits of that capability is a lower unemployment insurance rate.

Types of Employer/Employee Insurance that cover people are:
1. Accident and Health—sometimes called hospitalization, Blue Cross, etc.
2. Group Life
3. Pension (retirement)

Accident and Health insurance is sometimes fully paid for by the employer, sometimes fully paid for by the employee and sometimes the cost is shared by both. There are a wide variety of policies, from the familiar Blue Cross type which pays the cost of a hospital stay (with limitations) to the popular Major Medical type of coverage which is available from a number of insurance companies. Regardless of the policy type available and the method of paying the premium, this is probably the most widely used people insurance you will become involved with at your unit.

A unit manager should completely investigate the coverage provided and be able to intelligently answer an employee's questions about his "hospitalization" plan. Most companies provide a booklet which outlines the major points of the plan and should be available for each employee. This rarely answers all the questions asked by employees and the manager becomes the fountainhead of information on where to get what kind of question answered. The more you can learn about the plan provided at your location, the better off you will be.

Group Life insurance is just that, an insurance policy that pays off upon the death of the policyholder. Purchasing anything in a large quantity usually saves money and "grouping" life insurance coverage usually saves large amounts of money for the insurance company and, therefore, makes possible a lower rate for the policy holder. By spreading the risk of life insurance over a large number of employees, an employer is usually able to obtain a good price from an insurance company on the premium.

As with hospitalization insurance, group life insurance is paid for in various ways: by the company, the employee, or both.

Union Welfare insurance plans exist in some places where the foodservice workers are members of a trade union. These plans are negotiated with the employer as part of the union contract and are extremely varied. Some plans cover hospitalization, group life, pension and even state disability. Where a union plan exists, duplicate or alternate plans often exist for the non-union (exempt management) employees in the same location. It is not unusual to have two sets of insurance plans to be administered for the same location, one for the union personnel covered and a separate and different one for the non-union. There are also locations where more than one foodservice union represents the employees of the operation and they have different contracts and different welfare package plans.

Pension Insurance is a coverage that provides income upon retirement after a specific number of years with the employer and the attainment of a specific age, usually 55 or older. There are no standard patterns for this type of insurance and,therefore, there are many variations. Here again, the unit manager must investigate his own unit's policies and become familiar with them.

In all cases of "people" insurance where your employees are covered, they will look to the unit manager for advice and assistance. It is prudent to become as knowledgeable as possible in order to answer their questions. One need not be an insurance genius to become an insurance expert. You only have to learn where the answers can be obtained and go to that source for the required knowledge.

Property Insurance—Things

The public and products liability insurance previously discussed is basically a liability policy and the basis of insurance on "things" damaged by someone who works for you. The other property that is usually insured is the physical property of your operating unit. A comprehensive fire and theft policy usually provides the base for this coverage. Different companies you may work for will have differing opinions on the depth of coverage in dollars and the extent of coverage in property but, by and large, they will be quite similar in the technicalities of what they insure.

Policies of this type have a number of "extended coverage" services available for things like sprinkler leakage, boiler insurance, earthquake insurance, plate glass insurance and many more. In an industrial foodservice operation, many of these coverages are tied in with the policy covering the building, plant, factory, hospital or school where the foodservice is located. Usually a source is available and responsible for assuring that these forms of insurance are in effect and current and a little investigation on the part of the foodservice manager can obtain all the necessary insurance information he will need. Here again, you are an expert when you know where and how to find out what you need to know, when you need to know it.

Money Insurance

Insurance on the money for which you may be responsible is called a blanket crime policy. This is primarily a cash loss coverage that includes cash theft by your own employees, burglary and depositor forgery. Consider the amount of money you may have on hand at any one time and that is the maximum amount of insurance that is required on your money. A small foodservice with a $200 cash bank and $500 a day in sales does not require the amount of insurance that a large vending operation with thousands of dollars on hand at all times requires.

Recent crime waves in major cities, incidents of break-ins on vending machines in some plants and factories all tend to make insuring your money a very expensive proposition. In some areas, the degree of risk is so high that insurance companies will not provide coverage.

Filing Insurance Claims

All forms of insurance have "claim forms" to file for the claims being made on the insurance company. As a unit manager, you should be familiar with all the forms needed to make an insurance claim as may be required in your location. Different areas have different forms, but they all have one thing in common: they report all the facts the insurance company wants to know.

If you will review five or six such forms, you will get some understanding of how a claim form is prepared. Timely reporting of accidents, dismissals, thefts and other incidents that can cause a claim on your insurance is the best way to assure proper attention to the claim. A good manager becomes insurance conscious and by adding common sense to that quality he usually does the right thing in an emergency.

Summary

In summarizing general information about insurance, keep in mind that coverage is for people, things and money; the following limited list summarizes the different types and styles of coverage available under these headings:

PEOPLE INSURANCE
Customers
Public and Product Liability—covers products served and accidents on the premises
Employers (Mandated by law)
Workmen's Compensation—accidents on the job
State Disability—sickness or accident off the job
Employee Benefits
Accident and Health—hospitalization and major medical coverage
Group Life—Life insurance on a combined group basis
Pension Plan—Group Life covered with a retirement benefit
Welfare Plan—Usually a combined union package of health and life insurance

"THINGS" INSURANCE
Fire and Extended Coverage—Insures the things owned by the employer
Liability—Insures the things owned by others (see above)

MONEY INSURANCE
Fidelity and Forgery—A basic crime policy that insures you against loss of money by theft by your own employees or by outside burglary

Numerous sources exist for additional information about insurance in general and insurance for the foodservice operation in particular. The National Restaurant Association and the various state associations have a number of pamphlets about insurance in the food business. A good insurance agent or broker is perhaps the best source of information about types of insurance, other than those classed as employee benefits. Employee insurance is usually the responsibility of the company's personnel or industrial relations department. When in doubt or in need of information, such a contact will usually provide the answers.

Company Operation vs Caterer Operation

If you are directly employed by a business concern, school or hospital as their foodservice manager, all of your insurance coverages will be identical to those for the rest of the facility. If you are employed by a large enough organization, they will have their own insurance specialist who is available for assistance as you may need it. If yours is a smaller organization, they may utilize one or more insurance agents as outside sources with whom you may come in contact.

If you are employed by one of the major food and vending corporations, the policies of that corporation will be the policies of your operating unit, even though you are on the physical premises of a client company. The major food vending companies all carry very adequate insurance to assure their clients full coverage for any mishap by one of their employees. Most contracts to provide food and/or vending services specify that the catering company carry coverage in specific amounts and obey all state and federal laws regarding insurance for employees on the premises.

No matter how much you learn about insurance, you will have incidents arise that will be outside your scope of knowledge. As I said before:

The insurance expert is the manager who knows where to get the answers when he needs them.

XVI: Where Do You Go From Here?

This book has endeavored to assist an incumbent industrial foodservice manager or chef/manager in improving his management skills. It is also intended to serve as a "primer" for the foodservice student beginning his business career. Most of the information presented has been basic in nature with the "case for management" presented in basic terms. The use of case histories has been "borrowed" from the Harvard Graduate School of Business where this method is used to teach advanced management to graduate students; the use of case histories in this text, however, is simplified to a great degree.

It should be recognized that the combining of "management" and "industrial foodservice management" in this book has barely scratched the surface of the management knowledge that is required by any student or manager for a successful business career. Success in any business will only come after an individual has learned both the basics of his industry and the basics of management and then added his personal effort to combine and expand those basics to meet his own individual goals.

Chapter I ended with a look into the future of our industry. Without a doubt, some of the top companies in the industry today will, in the years to come, become some of the largest corporations on the American business scene. If you wish to share the opportunity that will evolve from this growth, this book will be only the beginning of your interest in and study of all phases of management.

Each chapter of this book could well require a complete book to cover its content completely. Each management topic in this book has previously had volumes of material published, much of it is immediately applicable to the individual manager or student. So then comes the question you should now ask yourself, "Where do I go from here?" Here are a few suggestions.

For the Student

If you are presently a student in a trade school or community college, you should be establishing both a short term and a long term personal goal for your educational and/or business accomplishment. Each student must make his own personal decision as to just how far he will extend his "formal" education and when he will place more emphasis on practical experience to achieve his goals.

Everyone is not a good classroom student. Some individuals can learn more in six months on the job than in six years in the classroom. Each student should reflect on the Biblical injunction, "know thyself" and, after careful consideration, should make his decision on when to leave the classroom and enter the industry.

A four-year college degree is always desirable but not always necessary. In the field of industrial foodservice management, a major portion of successful unit manager, district manager and higher management positions are held by men who do not have college degrees.

Trade school and community college graduates have set excellent records of accomplishment. Many of those with an impressive record of accomplishment have continued their education on an informal basis through seminars, personal reading and study and other similar individual effort. In most instances, special study of a management area at the time when it is demanding attention on the job is extremely rewarding and profitable.

Where then do you as a student "go from here——?"

1. To a job that can offer the opportunity you feel can further your ability, using your present education as a base

OR

2. To continuing your education toward a higher degree

OR

3. To a situation that combines both.

Seek a position that can help you make your decision whichever way (or both ways) that is the most desirable for your own personality, ability and personal goals.

As a Chef/Manager

If you are already employed in the combination worker-managerial position of chef/manager, you have displayed the ability to prepare food and be called a chef. You have also displayed sufficient management ability for an employer to pay you some portion of your salary for being a manager.

Should you prefer a career solely as a chef you should be seeking an opportunity to work with master chef's and learn their techniques of food preparation. Many industrial foodservice locations operate executive dining rooms that employ master chefs in their kitchens. Corporate and world headquarters of all major corporations provide their top executives with luncheon and other dining facilities that rival in quality famous hotels and luncheon clubs. Your aspiration should be to find an opportunity to work in such a facility and become its head chef. Sometimes reaching such a goal may require one step backward in order to take two steps forward but that may be the course to choose.

If as a chef/manager you make the decision to become a manager of a larger industrial foodservice unit that does not require that the manager also prepares the food, you should take a different view of your future plans since you already have the ability to prepare food, undoubtedly you also have the ability to supervise its preparation by others. In addition, basic skills in production, controls, budgeting and basic management have been reviewed in this book. You must now seek and accept a position that allows you to practice these skills and to supervise as well. That job could be as the manager of a middle-sized (up to 2000 population) unit or as the assistant manager of a large unit, population over 2000 and up to 6000 to 7000.

Where then do you as chef/manager "go from here——?"

1. To head chef of an executive dining room complex in the Corporate or World headquarters of a major corporation.

OR

2. To manager or assistant manager of a large, multi-faceted complex foodservice.

For the Unit Manager

If you are already a unit manager of an industrial foodservice, a different set of goals should be considered. Everyone wants to progress in life and for the manager of an industrial foodservice that means promotion to district manager, regional manager, division vice-president or even president of a small company. The first major step is the move from managing a single unit, which is in effect managing foodservice personnel, to managing multiple-units. At that time you will no longer be managing foodservice workers but managing foodservice managers and that is a whole new ball game. A completely new set of management skills is required to manage managers in any profession; a truly difficult set of skills is required to manage foodservice managers.

One approach to progressing along this route would be to obtain and review an organization chart of the company you are presently working for; after studying it, select the "ladder" you wish to climb. Establish a goal which you sincerely feel you are capable of achieving and plot the route necessary to achieving it. Realistically assess the management skill requirements at each level of management you must pass through to achieve your established goal, then plan how, where and when you will learn and master those management techniques and skills. The OBJECTIVE and P-O-A system to achieve an objective is one that can well be applied to yourself as an individual who wants to plan and achieve personal objectives. Try it—you may be surprised at how effectively you can use that type of thinking to evaluate your objective and plan a way to achieve it.

As a manager, "Where do you go from here——?"

As far as your own individual ambition will take you. There are no limits to accomplishments in the industrial foodservice field. The only limits are those you may place upon yourself, knowingly or unwittingly.

Business Magazines and Industry Associations

Two basic efforts that you as a student, chef/manager or manager should make is to read the various business magazines of our industry and to be active in at least one industry association.

There are many business magazines that publish articles on the various facets of foodservice management as well as providing a large amount of advertising by product and equipment suppliers. Since the actual cost of producing and distributing any magazine is borne by its advertisers, business magazines contain a large amount of advertising, much of which contains information of importance. The better publications have a good selection of advertising and editorial material and are well worth the time required to read them.

Industry or trade associations of many different styles and types exist in various parts of the country. Your suppliers are usually well informed about such groups. Since suppliers are constantly trying to create good relations with the operating management of the food-service industry, the trade association is a prime target for their public relations effort. If you question some of your more reliable and respected suppliers, you should be able to determine which organization or association you would like to join. If and when you do join an organization, keep in mind that any group is only as good as its members. Be an active member and you will get the most out of your association.

"Where do you go from here——?"

There are no limits, only yourself. Know thyself—and, guided by that knowledge, tomorrow for each of us in the industrial foodservice field is unlimited.

Glossary

A la Carte Prices—Prices for all items on a menu or menu sign that are not priced as combination meals but are priced individually.

Auxiliary Group—Volunteer non-profit work force.

Back of the House Employees—Production and preparation personnel.

Boarding (College)—"Live in" students who eat most of their meals in the college dining hall.

Budget—A projection of expected sales and operating costs.

Cash Bank—Amount of money put into each cash register to start the business day.

Central Kitchen—Single production area used for multiple service areas.

Chain of Command—The line of management responsibility established for the operation of an Industrial Foodservice or other organization.

Client—Plant, factory, hospital, school or other organization that employs a food management company.

Coffee Break—Time allotted to employees of a company, plant, factory or hospital to drink their coffee or partake of other refreshments.

Contracts—A legal agreement between a client company, school or hospital and a professional food management catering company.

Cycling—Repeating an action according to plan, i.e. to repeat the same menu in an established pattern.

Dietary Budget—Amount of money set aside for operation of foodservice department in a hospital or similar institution.

Dietitian—An individual qualified in or practicing the application of the principles of nutrition to foodservice; may also be engaged in foodservice administration.

EDP—Electronic Data Processing.

Federal W4 Form—Income Tax reporting form to declare number of dependents.

Food Cost—The ratio of dollars of food purchases to sales dollars, expressed as a percentage.

Format—Layout plan for a presentation, i.e., "Budget Format."

Geriatrics Department—Elderly medical ward; also used to describe older patients.

Gross—Total, i.e., total sales income.

Heating Ovens—Equipment used to heat or reheat prepared food.

Invoice—Bill for merchandise received.

Jacket File—Envelope type file folder used for personnel file history.

Job Descriptions—Breakdown of responsibilities and duties of a single position.

Job Breakdowns—Breakdown of tasks required to perform a specific duty.

Manager—One who plans and directs the work efforts of others toward a specific goal.

Man/Hours—Number of employee hours scheduled.

Manual Selling—A term used to connote the sale of "non-vended" foods.

Meal Cost—A term used to express food cost per meal in dollars as opposed to a percentage of sales.

Menu—Listing of items that are offered for sale on the premises where customer plans to eat.

Net—Total figure, minus costs, i.e., "Net" profit.

Patient Days—The average number of patients in a hospital per day; a figure used in estimating operating and budget information.

Payouts—Cash paid on demand.

Pediatrics Department—Children's medical ward.

Point of Sale—Place where edible food item is transferred to a customer.

Policy—Guidelines established for proper management.

Productivity—Measurable amount of work produced by the work force.

Profit or Loss Statement—A formal accounting that reports the results of sales and costs, usually produced monthly.

Pro Forma—A projection of sales, operating costs and expected profits for a new business venture.

Ratio—Comparison of one figure to another.

Snack Bar—An eating place that provides a light meal and also offers faster service.

Stops—Points of sale for a coffee cart or mobile food wagon.

Subsidize—To provide income other than that received from sales.

Subsidy—Amount of money paid to offset operating losses.

Task Breakdown—Breakdown of a job to make it possible to complete a specific duty successfully.

Theme—Style or type.

Unit Sale—Sale of a single item, i.e., "cups of coffee."

Vendor—Supplier.

Work Schedules—Schedule of tasks for the hours that an employee is assigned to work at his foodservice unit.